WHAT YOU
REALLY NEED
TO KNOW
FOR THE
SECOND HALF
OF LIFE

WHAT YOU
REALLY NEED
TO KNOW
FOR THE
SECOND HALF
OF LIFE

PROTECT YOUR FAMILY!

Published by Advantage, Charleston, South Carolina.
Member of Advantage Media Group.

ADVANTAGE is a registered trademark and the Advantage colophon is a trademark of Advantage Media Group, Inc.

Printed in the United States of America.

ISBN: 978-1-59932-469-2
LCCN: 2015952496

This publication is designed to provide accurate and authoritative information in regard to the subject matter covered. It is sold with the understanding that the publisher is not engaged in rendering legal, accounting, or other professional services. If legal advice or other expert assistance is required, the services of a competent professional person should be sought.

Advantage Media Group is proud to be a part of the Tree Neutral® program. Tree Neutral offsets the number of trees consumed in the production and printing of this book by taking proactive steps such as planting trees in direct proportion to the number of trees used to print books. To learn more about Tree Neutral, please visit www.treeneutral.com. To learn more about Advantage's commitment to being a responsible steward of the environment, please visit www.advantagefamily.com/green

Advantage Media Group is a publisher of business, self-improvement, and professional development books and online learning. We help entrepreneurs, business leaders, and professionals share their Stories, Passion, and Knowledge to help others Learn & Grow. Do you have a manuscript or book idea that you would like us to consider for publishing? Please visit advantagefamily.com or call 1.866.775.1696.

DISCLAIMER

This book does not constitute and should not be treated as legal advice. The authors do not assume responsibility for your reliance on or use of the information in this book. You should contact a senior estate planning or elder law attorney for advice regarding your particular circumstances. Furthermore, the authors do not assume responsibility for any errors or omissions in this book. Although every effort has been made to assure the accuracy of the information in this book at the time of the writing of this book, laws and regulations are constantly changing, so you should contact a senior estate planning or elder law attorney before taking any action with regard to your estate and long-term health-care planning.

PREFACE

I had the pleasure of coordinating the writing of this book and hand selecting this group of leading elder care attorneys from across the United States. It was an honor to work with these leading lawyers, and I want to thank each of them for sharing their knowledge and experience with the readers of this book.

—Julieanne E. Steinbacher,

Certified as an Elder Law Attorney

by the National Elder Law Foundation

ABOUT JULIEANNE

Julieanne E. Steinbacher is the founding shareholder of Steinbacher, Stahl, Goodall & Yurchak, an elder care and special needs planning law firm with locations in Williamsport, PA and State College, PA. She is certified as an Elder Law Attorney by the National Elder Law Foundation. Her law practice focuses on estate and long-term care planning. As an attorney, her goal is to provide a bridge between legal services and the aging network.

Julie belongs to the National Association of Elder Law Attorneys (NAELA); Academy of Special Needs Planners (ASNP); Wealth Counsel, LLC; and Elder Counsel, LLC. She has been selected as a Presidential Who's Who and approved to the National Association of Professional Women. Additionally, Julie is an accredited attorney by the Department of Veteran Affairs and may prepare, present, and prosecute claims for the department.

Prior to becoming an attorney, Julie was employed by AARP and as a social worker at a nursing home. She has extensive lecturing experience as a speaker for Pennsylvania State University Tax Institutes and Tax Week, Pennsylvania Institute of Certified Public Accountants (PICPA), National Association of Tax Professionals—PA Chapter, Pennsylvania Society of Public Accountants (PSPA), Pennsylvania Bar Institute's Elder Law Institute, Pennsylvania Bar Association's Annual Meeting, Back to Basics, Tax Pro Seminars, and the University of Illinois. In addition, she has conducted numerous local seminars for various organizations.

Julie is the president of Estate & Long Term Care Planning, Inc., a company that provides continuing education for professionals in Pennsylvania and coaching for attorneys throughout the United States. She has written materials published by the University of Illinois on estates, trusts, and taxation. She also has published materials in various newsletters and newspapers. Julie and her law partner, Adrianne J. Stahl, Esquire, authored two books about trusts, entitled *Pennsylvania Trust Guide* (Editions I and II) and *Pennsylvania Special Needs Planning Guide* published by George T. Bisel Company, Inc. Most recently, Julie and her law partner, Adrianne J. Stahl, joined by nine other leading elder law attorneys from across the nation, coauthored *Protect Your Family! Don't Write a Blank Check to the Nur$ing Home*, a collaborative writing, broken down in layman's terms, offering readers the essential tools and knowledge for effective long-term care planning.

Julie's favorite quote is "It's not enough for a great nation to have added new years to life. Our objective must be to add new life to years," by John Fitzgerald Kennedy, thirty-fifth president of the United States.

TABLE OF CONTENTS

PLANNING AHEAD GIVES
YOU THE OPPORTUNITY
TO MEET GOALS YOU HAVE SET
FOR YOURSELF AND YOUR FAMILY.

CHAPTER 1

SENIOR ESTATE PLANNING: PLANNING FOR THE SECOND HALF OF LIFE

Janis A. Carney,

Certified Elder Law Attorney
by the National Elder Law Foundation,
Certified Specialist Estate Planning Trust and Probate Law by the
State Bar of California Board of Legal Specialization,
and Accredited Attorney by the Veterans Administration

§ 1.1. The Four Stages of Estate Planning
    § 1.1.1. The Young Family Estate Planning Stage
    § 1.1.2. The Mature Family Estate Planning Stage
    § 1.1.3. The Senior Estate Planning Stage
    § 1.1.4. The Elder Crisis Estate Planning Stage
§ 1.2. The Senior Estate Plan: An Overview of the Details
    § 1.2.1. Social Security Planning
    § 1.2.2. Medicare Planning
    § 1.2.3. Senior and Long-Term Care Housing Options

§ 1.1.
THE FOUR STAGES OF ESTATE PLANNING

Planning ahead gives us the opportunity to meet the objectives we have set for ourselves and our families. We have all heard the old adage: *Failing to plan is planning to fail.* Certainly, there is some luck involved in reaching our life goals, but luck alone is never enough. The path to fulfilling our dreams is making and following a good plan.

Traditionally, the primary goal of estate planning has been to meet our objectives about what will happen when we die. It focused principally on protecting our family from the financially devastating circumstances that may arise due to our death. It was about trying to predict and plan for the myriad of possible events and circumstances that might befall our family in dealing with the future without us in it. Rarely does the traditional, simple "I love you" will, leaving everything directly to our spouse, provide the best protection for our family. Rather, most of us need a comprehensive and well-conceived estate plan that we adjust over the years as our circumstances change—a plan that matures as we and our family members mature. The needs and goals of our estate planning should track and respond to the stage we are at in our life.

For estate planning purposes, there are four separate stages in an adult life. Good planning at each stage reflects the typical psychosocial and financial issues and concerns present at that point in our life. At each stage, our planning must recognize and overcome the new and often changing obstacles to achieving our goals for ourselves and our families.

§ 1.1.1.
The Young Family Estate Planning Stage

The first estate planning stage is for those of us in our early family years. This is typically between the ages 20 and 40 when we are new in our careers, have a young family, and possibly have purchased our first home. Our young family estate planning often involves having a large life insurance policy to provide some financial security for our family and naming guardians for our minor children in case we die suddenly. Naturally, we want to minimize the hassle for our family of dealing with our estate, but since our estate is often fairly modest, this is usually not a big concern. Also, for most of us at this stage of our life, our estate is not yet large enough that we have to do much, if any, planning to avoid estate or death taxes. But, what we are concerned about is how our young family will go on to thrive without our personal and financial support and participation. Who will raise our children? How will our children be protected and provided for? Will our spouse and children be forced to sell their home? Will our children be okay if our spouse remarries? The focus of a good estate plan for the early family years must address what will happen if we die far too soon.

§ 1.1.2.
The Mature Family Estate Planning Stage

The second stage of estate planning comes in our middle years, usually when we are between the ages of 40 and 60. At this point, we and our family have matured. Our children are usually grown, and we are amassing resources and achieving whatever financial success we will have in our life. So, the mature family estate planning stage naturally focuses more on how to minimize estate and death taxes and how to simplify the process of passing our estate to our family upon our death. Sometimes, if we are in a second or third marriage, it also involves issues of trying to ensure family harmony and perceived fairness. How do we include our children from a prior marriage? Although grown, are our children really mature and competent adults? Will they squander their inheritance or lose it to a divorce or debt problems? Do we have some children who need or deserve more help than others? If so, what will happen to our children's relationships with each other if we adjust for such circumstances? These are some of the concerns that arise when we create an estate plan for our mature family. Of course, like the planning for our early family years, the focus during these years is mostly on what will happen to our family and estate if we die suddenly.

§ 1.1.3.
The Senior Estate Planning Stage

The third stage of planning typically begins with the start of our senior years at about age 60 and lasts well into our 80s or until we become ill. This stage, which is coming to be called "senior estate planning," again addresses what will happen when we die. But notice the subtle change in focus. It is no longer what will happen "if we die" too soon or suddenly. It is now "when we die," for, at this point, we have begun to accept that it will eventually happen. Further, our family is by now usually well settled. We are no longer primarily worried about how they will go on without our support and protection if we suddenly die. Of course, our planning at this stage still needs to minimize any estate and death taxes and make sure our estate passes to our family with as little hassle as possible. But, what we are becoming more concerned about at this stage is planning for our own second half of life.

More than what will happen when we die, senior estate planning addresses what will happen if we don't die. That is, our planning at this stage needs to address planning for our life, not just for our death. We are concerned about how to maintain our lifestyle and protect the quality of our life. How do we maintain our present good health? How do we insure that we can continue to get good health care? Will we have enough income and savings to cover our everyday expenses and not outlive our money? Will we be able to remain independent in our own homes as we age? We are apprehensive about Social Security and Medicare. What options do we have under these programs, and when must we sign up? What will happen if we don't sign up for a program on time?

While not yet high on the list of concerns for most seniors, we should also be planning at this stage for the catastrophic effects of becoming chronically ill and needing long-term health care. How will we deal with the loss of our good health and independence? Will we be able to afford the care we need? What options will we have if we or our spouse needs care? What happens if our spouse loses capacity or also needs care? Will we be able to depend on our family or friends to help us over the long years of our decline and through the intense period of our complete incapacity? Do we want to depend on them? What if our care is literally killing our spouse, ruining our children's marriages, or financially devastating our family? Should we be buying long-term care insurance now, just in case? What are the odds of us needing long-term health care? What public assistance is available to help pay for long-term care? What do we need to do to qualify for assistance? Is there a way to preserve our homes and assets for our family if we do need care?

What if we lose the mental capacity to make decisions for ourselves? Will someone have the power to make health-care decisions for us and handle our financial affairs? Will they know what we would want? What if we are unable to recognize that we need help or are unwilling to accept it? How can we plan to make sure that we do not become a victim of physical and/or financial abuse?

In comparison to dealing with these issues, estate planning for what will happen when we die is easy. It is no wonder that most seniors don't want to address these concerns. It is much preferable to just stick our heads in the sand, as the saying goes; however, the only thing harder than senior estate planning is elder crisis estate planning.

§ 1.1.4.
The Elder Crisis Estate Planning Stage

Elder crisis estate planning is hardly planning at all. It is more the process of responding to a present and ongoing situation that is often the single most devastating crisis of a person's life. Almost always, the elder crisis involves how to provide and pay for long-term care. It often means dealing with an angry elder who may be withdrawing and suffering from severe depression due to the loss of good health and independence. It can also involve protecting a failing elder from abusers even within their own family.

Elder crisis estate planning typically arises for elders starting at the age of 80. However, it may occur many years earlier due to the early onset of some cognitive decline caused by diseases such as Alzheimer's, Parkinson's, alcoholism, and diabetes or from the effects of a stroke.

At the point in which elder crisis estate planning is needed, it is way too late to obtain long-term care insurance. It is also often too late for elders to participate in the planning due to loss of capacity, for they no longer are able to understand and execute documents such as trusts, powers of attorney, and advance health-care directives or to transfer assets to preserve them for their family. For those who have lost capacity, we must look to what, if any, prior planning documents the elder had executed and the powers provided in those documents.

Did the elder give his spouse or children the ability to take the steps needed to qualify him for public benefits? What can be done at this late date to preserve the elder's assets for his care and for his spouse and children? If he has long-term care insurance, what will it cover and for how long? How much more will be needed to cover the full cost of the elder's care? Does the elder's family have the ability to liquidate assets to pay for the elder's care? If needed, can the elder obtain a reverse mortgage against his residence to keep him in his home and pay for in-home caregivers? How do we find quality care-givers and avoid the horror stories about caregivers who steal the elder's valuables or affections? What other community resources and care options are available to the elder at this point? Will we need to have a guardian or conservator appointed by the court to make health decisions for the elder, to handle his financial affairs, or to protect him from elder abuse? If so, can and will the court even consider giving the guardian or conservator the authority to do planning to qualify the elder for public benefits?

§ 1.2.
THE SENIOR ESTATE PLAN: AN OVERVIEW OF THE DETAILS

The senior estate plan, which is the focus of this book, needs to include much more than the mere estate planning documents that spell out what happens when the senior dies. The plan should also address the other issues concerning the senior.

§ 1.2.1.
Social Security Planning

For the senior who is not yet age 65, the senior estate plan should contain a report on the senior's options for taking Social Security and guidance on getting professional assistance in evaluating the options.

The report should include information about the Social Security rules and how to elect the option with the optimum payout over the senior's life expectancy. There are a number of techniques that can be used, especially by a married senior. Whether to take benefits beginning at age 62 or at age 66 or to wait until age 70 requires an evaluation of what other income the senior will have at the time and the tax consequences. Of course, it also requires a guess as to how long the senior might live. Although this often requires a crystal ball, there may be health issues and a family medical history that would be helpful in making an informed decision. If the senior and his spouse are approximately the same age they may be able to use a technique called "filing and suspending" in order to maximize the total amount they would receive provided they each lived out their life expectancy. There are chapters of this book devoted to Social Security planning and achieving a secure retirement, which you should read to get more details about Social Security benefits.

§ 1.2.2.
Medicare Planning

Medicare is the health-care benefit we become entitled to when we turn 65 years of age. We also become eligible for Medicare 24 months after we qualify for Social Security disability insurance if we become totally and permanently disabled before the age of 62. To get coverage under Medicare, we (or our spouse) must have earned sufficient credits to qualify for Social Security or pay a monthly premium. Although most government workers, teachers, and railroad employees will receive a pension instead of Social Security, they too generally qualify for Medicare.

There are four different parts to the Medicare system: Part A, Part B, Part C, and Part D. Part A, known as "hospitalization," covers hospital, nursing home (for limited rehabilitation), and hospice benefits, subject to certain deductibles and copayments. There is no premium for Part A coverage if the individual (or his/her spouse) is eligible for Social Security or other government benefits mentioned above, as this is the coverage paid for by deductions from the recipient's (or his/her spouse's) salary during his/her working years. If the individual (or his/her spouse) has not qualified for Social Security or similar government benefits, he/she may be able to purchase Medicare Part A benefits by paying a coverage premium. However, in this author's experience, the amount of this premium is very high.

Part B, which is known as "medical," covers doctors' bills, lab tests, ambulance trips, durable medical equipment, and certain medications, such as those used in chemotherapy. The premium charged for Part B is based on the recipient's income. Most seniors whose principal income is only Social Security pay $104.90 per month for Part B, which is automatically deducted from their monthly Social Security payments.

The reader should also know that there are private insurance plans available that cover the gaps in coverage, for example, plans that pay the deductibles and copayments for covered services, under Medicare Part A and Part B. The government has regulated these private insurance "Medigap" plans and classified the coverage under them as plans A through N, so that an individual will get the same coverage under a particular plan letter, regardless of the insurance company from which they buy the coverage.

Medicare Part C, called the Medicare Advantage Plan, provides the recipient with the option of taking his/her Medicare under a private health maintenance organization (HMO), preferred provider organization (PPO), private fee-for-service plan, special needs plan, or Medicare Medical Savings Account Plan. Some, but not necessarily all, of these options are available in all areas of the country, and they may (but are not required to) provide prescription drug coverage. The recipient must pay the monthly Part B premium (described above) plus an extra Part C premium determined by the private company that will be providing the recipient with his/her Medicare Advantage Plan services. The coverage under a Medicare Advantage Plan must be at least as good as the coverage available under straight Medicare Part A plus Part B.

Medicare Part D covers the recipient's pharmaceutical costs, subject to deductibles and copayments. These benefits are provided by private insurance companies that charge a premium based on the coverage selected by the recipient. Each year, the insurance company must provide a list of the medications it will cover for the following year so that each person can compare and decide on the coverage plan that best fits his/her needs.

Although Parts B and D are optional, there are very significant late enrollment penalties imposed for individuals who do not sign up for them when they are first eligible to do so and who wish to get them later.

§ 1.2.3.
Senior and Long-Term Care Housing Options

It is important for seniors and elders today to understand the care and housing options available to them.

Most seniors hope to be able to remain in their home as long as they live. This has become known as "aging in place." Certainly, the healthy, vigorous, independent, and competent senior should be able to stay home as long as he/she wishes, barring financial problems. However, once a chronic illness or disability sets in, some sort of in-home care may be necessary for the senior to remain safely at home. In-home caregivers may be family members or professional caregivers, hired independently or through an in-home care agency. Seniors and their families must be very careful when hiring an independent caregiver, as this is the source of most stories told about caregivers who stole from the senior or even manipulated and stole the senior's affections away from his/her family, sometimes even marrying the senior, in order to get control of the senior's wealth. It is highly recommended that a "full-service" home-care agency be retained to provide the caregivers. Be sure that the agency is bonded, handles all of the employment responsibilities for the employee-caregivers and does criminal background checks on all employees. The cost of care in the home will depend on the number of hours of care provided. At some point, the cost to stay at home with caregivers exceeds the cost of care in all but the most expensive of assisted living or skilled nursing facilities. In addition, it could become impossible, or at least impractical, to stay in the home due to the level of care needed and/or the lack of adaptability of the home to the care requirements (such as accessibility for a wheelchair).

In most communities, there are professional elder care coordinators (ECC) or geriatric care managers (GCM) who can do a needs assessment and care plan for the senior. These plans address the medical, physical, psychosocial, and economic condition of the elder and the family. The ECC/GCM provides information about community resources as well as guidance in selecting trustworthy care providers and can provide ongoing oversight of the senior and the caregivers. This service may be invaluable in helping the senior stay safely at home when family live far away or when the senior is unwilling to allow family to become involved with his/her care.

Another option for the senior who may not be quite as hale and hearty, but who is still competent and relatively independent, is the independent living facility (ILF), sometimes called a senior living community. Here, the senior lives in his/her own apartment, which may be a studio or a one or two bedroom unit. The facility/community provides delicious and nutritious meals (sometimes only lunch and dinner) in a common dining room, transportation to local shopping and doctors' offices, opportunities to participate in many social activities in and outside of the facility/community, and, most importantly, some protective oversight to make sure that the senior is doing well. When the senior begins to fail or if the senior suffers an injury or becomes ill, the facility will call the family for emergency medical services. This level of facility normally does not have a nurse on staff and, even if it does have a nurse, provides no medical services or hands-on personal assistance with the basic activities of daily living. However, some ILFs allow the residents to independently hire caregivers to provide such services.

The next housing/care option is some type of residential care facility for the elderly (RCFE). These include the small (usually six-bed) board and care facilities, the larger assisted living facilities, and dementia care facilities. The services provided at this level vary widely and depend in great part on the needs of the senior. Usually, seniors in a RCFE require some assistance with the basic activities of daily living and/or close protective oversight to make sure they are safe.

Many dementia patients can do well, at least for a time, in the smaller board and care facility but usually require more care and oversight than can be provided by the normal larger assisted living facility. These patients typically require the special services of a dementia facility in order to provide the level of staffing and special activities needed to attend to the cognitive deficits of the dementia patient, and the secure perimeter needed to keep the dementia patient safe. Some regular assisted living facilities include a special "memory unit" part of their facility to care for the needs of the dementia patient.

The RCFE staff generally consists of unlicensed caregivers and rarely includes a nurse as, like the ILF, they usually cannot provide any medical services to the patients. There are two exceptions. One is the board and care facility that is owned and operated by a registered nurse or doctor, where the nurse/doctor provides the medical services. Often, a diabetic patient who has cognitive problems and needs someone to do glucose checks and give him insulin injections must find such a facility. Also, some RCFEs that have more than the minimum level of staffing for the normal RCFE license may be able to obtain a "hospice licensing waiver" to care for a patient needing a higher level of care if the patient is terminal and on hospice care.

A skilled nursing facility, sometimes called a "nursing home," provides temporary and/or long-term nursing level care. The patient in skilled nursing must need some medical care. The condition that requires such care may be physical, such as a broken hip or an open wound, or may be cognitive, such as a stroke or an advanced level of dementia. Patients who are there for rehabilitation due to some medical condition will generally stay only so long as they need and continue to improve from physical, occupational, and/or speech therapy. Patients who require ongoing custodial care must have some medical need requiring care such as a chronic illness or condition. These patients are normally deemed to be long-term care patients and may be in a separate area of the nursing home from the rehabilitation patients. Like the RCFEs, some nursing homes have separate units that provide for the special needs of patients with advanced dementia.

§ 1.2.4.
Financial Planning: How Do I Make My Money Last?

Financial planning is the process of creating a detailed strategy, tailored to the individual's specific situation, to meet his/her specific financial goals and objectives. For most people, financial plans during their working years focus on growing wealth and include a level of risk that the market may swing down. However, the risk inherent in such plans may be unacceptable to seniors who have little time to recover from a substantial financial loss and no ability to replace investments that were lost. Therefore, financial planning for most seniors focuses on controlling the risk involved in the seniors' investments in order to preserve, rather than accumulate, wealth. They want to make sure that their money lasts at least as long as they live. However, where to get help to make this happen can be confusing for seniors.

There are many financial professionals who claim to have special expertise in working with and creating plans for seniors. Some of the "senior specialist" financial planning designations require extensive training and experience working with and on the needs of seniors and may take years to obtain. Others may be obtained with very little effort or experience and may be used to exploit and even defraud seniors. The reader is encouraged to research the certification requirements touted by anyone claiming to be some sort of senior specialist advisor.

Check out the information about "senior specialists and advisors" provided by the U.S. Securities and Exchange Commission on its website (www.sec.gov). Additional information can be found on the website for the new federal consumer financial watchdog agency, the Consumer Financial Protection Bureau (www.consumerfinance.gov), and its newly created Office of Financial Protection for Older Americans that is charged with addressing financial issues of the large and rapidly expanding community of seniors in America.

---

§ 1.2.5.
Preplanning for the Cost of Long-Term Care

As part of a complete financial plan, every senior should consider how he/she will pay for long-term care if needed in the future. There are really only four ways to pay for the cost of long-term custodial care: private pay, long-term care insurance, Medicaid, and VA benefits.

Private pay means using the senior's income and savings, as well as liquidating any other available assets, to pay for the care. Certainly, if the need for care lasts longer and/or the cost is greater than what was budgeted for, the senior's ability to privately pay for care may exhaust all available assets. Further, many seniors strongly desire to leave something, especially their home, for their family when they are gone. If all of the senior's assets must be spent on long-term care, the senior's most fervent wish to help his family may not be possible.

Many seniors who are young and healthy enough to qualify may decide to purchase a long-term care insurance policy to pay for their care. However, as such policies can vary widely, it is important that the senior research what coverage any policy he/she is considering offers and under what circumstance it will pay for care. It is also important to compare the terms of different policies and the policies of different insurance companies to understand their terms. Finally, to make sure that the insurance company is financially strong enough to be there if and when the individual needs it to pay for care in the future, it is important to evaluate and compare the financial stability of the insurance companies offering the policies. In most states, it is now possible to obtain a "partnership" long-term care policy that must meet certain minimum standards set by the state and that allows the insured individual to protect some of his/her assets from the Medicaid spend down ordinarily required before he/she can qualify for long-term care benefits.

Medicaid is a combined federal-state partnership program established under title XIX of the U.S. code that provides medical coverage to qualified low-income individuals. In order to obtain federal Medicaid funds, a state must establish and maintain its own benefit program, which it can call by any name it desires. While most states merely call their program "Medicaid," others call it something else. For example, in California it is called "Medi-Cal," in Tennessee it is "TennCare," and in Maine it is "MaineCare." In order to qualify for Medicaid benefits to pay for long-term care, individuals must be financially needy. Further, Medicaid generally will only pay for patients who are in a skilled nursing facility. However, some states now offer Medicaid benefits under various nursing-home waiver programs that may provide assistance for patients who need a skilled nursing home level of care but who desire to be cared for at home or, in some states, in an assisted living facility. Due to the variations between the states, the reader is strongly advised to consult with an elder law attorney in his/her state to determine the eligibility rules and benefits available through his/her state's Medicaid program.

Elder law and senior estate planning attorneys are also able to help clients preplan for how they will pay for their future long-term care. The details of such planning will vary from person to person depending on his/her financial circumstances and that of his/her family. Planning for long-term care involves a thorough under-standing of the senior's finances and health concerns, as well as a comprehensive knowledge of complex rules for eligibility under that state's Medicaid program. It also requires an evaluation of the tax and other consequences of any proposed plan and what benefits are available under the state's Medicaid program. Many preplans include the creation of various types of irrevocable trusts to preserve the senior's assets for his/her family in the event long-term care is needed. Such trusts often contain very sophisticated and legally technically complex provisions that most normal estate planning attorneys, who do not include long-term care planning as part of their practice, would not normally use in their trusts. Some preplans for long-term care may also include the purchase of life insurance, often held in an irrevocable trust created just to hold such a policy, to protect the surviving spouse by replacing the assets used to pay for the ill spouse's long-term care. The authors of this book are all elder law and senior estate planning attorneys in their respective states and possess the experience and knowledge needed to help their clients, who are leading-edge boomers, seniors, or elders, plan for their long-term care.

§ 1.2.6.
Planning for Alternative Decision Making If I Lose Capacity

Giving authority to someone else to make decisions for an individual, if and when the individual loses the capacity to do so for himself, is part of any sound estate plan and may be vital for long-term care planning. In every state, it is possible to create documents to do this.

A durable power of attorney (DPA) is used to give the power to someone to make financial decisions, manage property, and handle financial transactions for the individual who created the DPA. The person who gives this power is known as the "principal," and the person who is given the power is called the "attorney-in-fact." The powers granted by the principal in a DPA can be limited to only specific powers or can be general; that is, they can be broad powers. However, most states have statutes now that state that certain powers, including the power to make gifts; change beneficiaries under retirement plans and life insurance policies; and create, revoke, or amend a trust must be expressly set forth in the DPA document. As these powers are the ones most needed to do long-term care planning in many cases, the typical general power of attorney usually will not be sufficient. Therefore, the person wishing to give authority to his/her attorney-in-fact to do long-term care planning, if and when needed, should specifically discuss this concern with his/her attorney and, perhaps, seek advice from an elder law attorney in his state.

All states also now allow individuals to create some type of instrument to give alternate decision-making authority over health and personal care decisions. However, exactly what powers can be given and which document is needed to give those powers varies widely from state to state.

Some states allow health-care powers to be included in the same document with financial powers, and other states require them to be in a separate document. Also, some states allow the health-care power-of-attorney document to include the individual's wishes about end-of-life decisions and others require it to be in a separate document, often called a "living will." And, some states call the agent for health care a "health-care surrogate" and call the document giving authority to the surrogate a "health-care proxy." Finally, there are now various forms of these documents available online that may suit the particular individual's wishes better than the standard form in his/her state. However, the person thinking of using one of these should first consult an elder law or senior estate planning attorney in his/her state to make sure the desired document will satisfy the legal requirements in his/her state.

§ 1.2.7.
Planning for What Happens to My Stuff When I Die

At its end, all estate and long-term planning must accomplish what the individual wanted to have happen to his assets when he dies. Most people understand this to be the function of a last will and testament, which, of course, it is. However, there are several other ways to provide for the disposition of assets at death.

A "beneficiary designation" is typically used on life insurance and annuity contracts. When completed properly, such a designation will leave the death benefits associated with the contract to whomever the owner named. Beneficiary designations are also used for retirement accounts, such as IRAs and 401(k)s, to leave anything left in the account at the owner's death to his desired beneficiary. This is known as providing for the disposition of the asset by contract.

"Joint tenancy with rights of survivorship" is a way of titling an asset, which provides that upon the death of one joint tenant, the remaining joint tenant(s) gets the asset by virtue of the title. Joint tenancy is commonly used for financial accounts and sometimes for the title to real estate, as an easy way to avoid probate of the asset.

"Payable-on-death" (POD) and "transfer-on-death" (TOD) are ways to leave a financial account to a specified individual at the account owner's death. If the account owner's sole objective is to avoid probate of the financial account at his death, this may be safer than the joint tenancy account since the death beneficiary will not have access to the account during the account owner's lifetime. A few states now also allow a similar designation on real property.

A trust, whether it is a revocable living trust or an irrevocable trust, will also provide for who is to have the asset after some event. In a revocable living trust, this event is normally the death of the grantor of the trust: that is, the person who created and funded the trust. In states where probating an estate is an expensive and time consuming process, the use of a living trust is desired for the flexibility and control it gives to the grantor during his lifetime. Irrevocable trusts are created for numerous tax, asset protection, and personal reasons, including sometimes to preserve assets for the grantor's family in the event the grantor needs long-term care. The terms of irrevocable trusts vary depending on the purpose of the trust. However, all trusts must designate one or more beneficiaries for whom the trust was created as well as how and when the trust estate is to be used for or distributed to the beneficiary(ies).

In some states, titling an asset owned by a married couple as "Community Property" or "Tenancy by the Entirety" may cause it to automatically pass, by operation of the title, to the surviving spouse on the death of the first spouse. The effect of such titling is very state specific, so the reader is especially cautioned to check with an attorney in his/her state.

Although it may be possible to use one or more of the above forms to designate who should receive a specific asset at an individual's death, some may be better for tax or other reasons in any given state. An attorney who focuses on senior estate planning or elder law in the state where the individual lives and any state where the individual owns real property should be consulted to make sure that the arrangements will accomplish the intended result and will not subject the property or the beneficiary(ies) to additional taxes or create other problems for the individual's estate.

The other chapters in this book will explore and explain the issues and options involved in senior estate planning for the second half of life. They will go into more detail about many of the topics raised in this chapter and present planning options to help seniors get their legal and financial ducks in a row for the future.

For more information, visit the website of

Carney Elder Law

at **www.carneyelderlaw.com**

WHY SHOULD WE HIRE AN
ESTATE PLANNING ATTORNEY
WHEN WE CAN USE BOB'S
ATTORNEY FROM WORK?

CHAPTER 2

THE HIGH PRICE OF FAILURE: THE UNNECESSARY COSTS UPON YOUR FAMILY, FINANCES, AND EMOTIONAL AND PHYSICAL HEALTH

Michael L. Brumbaugh, Esquire
Accredited Attorney by the Veterans Administration

§ 2.1.
INTRODUCTION

Melvin and Myrtle Antt and Bob and Betty Hopper were great friends who lived next door to each other. They had a lot in common. Melvin and Bob worked together in the local factory. Myrtle and Betty both stayed home raising the children until they started school. Once the kids were in school, Myrtle and Betty both found jobs outside of the home. The Antts and the Hoppers each managed to take good care of their families while at the same time putting aside money for retirement.

After starting a family, Melvin and Myrtle created an estate plan. With the help of their attorney, they discussed their desires and concerns and came up with a plan to achieve their goals. Among their goals were making sure they took care of each other and making sure their children were taken care of if something happened to the two of them.

When the Antts were nearing retirement, they determined they needed a different kind of attorney to meet their changing goals. They located a senior estate planning attorney.

During a Sunday afternoon barbeque, Melvin and Myrtle asked their neighbors, the Hoppers, if they had a good senior estate planning attorney because if they didn't, they'd be glad to share the name of the attorney they were using. Bob said they were fine. They'd had the attorney, covered by the prepaid legal plan provided by Bob's work, draw up their wills, and everything was taken care of and under control. Although Bob and Betty Hopper would never say anything to their good friends, they both thought the Antts were foolishly spending money on an attorney when they could use the free attorney provided through work. This surprised them, as they generally found the Antts to be quite wise.

As more time passed, Melvin and Myrtle periodically met with their elder care attorney and updated their plan as their needs changed. Their goals now also included taking care of grandchildren and making sure they never "ended up in probate." They also discussed their desire to be able to live at home as long as possible even if they started needing assistance.

Meanwhile, the Hoppers updated their wills with their free legal plan attorney before Bob retired. The attorney advised the Hoppers they should have health-care and financial power-of-attorney documents put in place as well without any real explanation as to why they were needed. As the Hoppers mistakenly thought they'd be giving up control if they created such power-of-attorney documents, they decided to wait and have them done when they needed them.

When Melvin had a stroke, it was a difficult time for the family. However, Melvin had progressed through rehabilitation well and went back home. Years before, Melvin and Myrtle had moved to a house with everything on one floor that was handicap accessible. Now, even though Melvin needed to use a walker, and his right hand didn't work as well as it used to, Melvin was able to get around the house and even open and shut the doors because they had doorknobs designed for someone who might have issues using their hands. The yard, grounds, and exterior maintenance needs of their house were taken care of by the association where they lived. The children visited frequently, helping out some, but mostly visiting and spending quality time with their parents. Myrtle had a housekeeping service come in several times a week.

As the years passed and Myrtle quit driving and Melvin needed more help, the people who provided housekeeping began helping Melvin with his bathing and dressing and drove the Antts to their appointments. They even did the shopping for them. These home care services were paid for by insurance they had purchased years ago as part of their senior estate plan.

When Melvin passed, the funeral service went smoothly with Melvin being dressed in his favorite outfit and some of his favorite verses being read at the ceremony. Myrtle soon after moved to an assisted living facility that she and Melvin and the children had looked at quite some time ago. Their daughter, Jane, who had financial power of attorney, took care of selling their house. The assisted living facility's cost was paid by Myrtle's long-term care insurance.

Myrtle enjoyed the companionship at her new home. There was a great chef on staff and plenty of activities for her to participate in and new hobbies to try. She was glad that she and Melvin had included their children in their senior estate plan over the years. She felt comfortable that Jane and her attorney knew her wishes and that they could continue implementing a plan they had worked on and updated over the years. She knew the children would be able to take care of the financial and health-care decisions that would need to be made if a time ever came when she couldn't handle making them herself. Myrtle felt a sense of relief knowing she and Melvin had provided the children the legal authority to make such decisions. She also knew that with the plan they had created, even if she lived many years in assisted living and then a nursing home, she would be well provided for and assets would still be preserved for their children. Finally, she was satisfied that when she passed, her senior estate plan would provide her with the type of funeral she wanted and pass her remaining assets to her children, outside of probate, in a fair manner, following her and Melvin's wishes.

Betty remembered how she and Bob had thought the Antts were silly for moving to that "old folks" development with the high association fees that paid for taking care of the yard and snow removal and outside maintenance among other things. She thought about that often as she lugged the laundry up and down the steps between the upstairs bedroom and the laundry room on the first floor.

Betty no longer had to take much clothing upstairs for Bob. Ever since his health had failed and he could no longer get up and down the stairs, he stayed on the first floor and slept on the hospital bed they had put in the living room. It was difficult on her and the children getting Bob in and out of the tub. He had already fallen once, and she had hurt her back helping lift him. They had looked into hiring outside help, but it seemed like a waste of money when she could still do most things and at least some of the kids, mostly their daughter, Sarah, were able and willing to help when they could.

While Bob was still able to get around, they went to the bank to add their son, Frank, to their bank accounts so he could help write out checks and go back and forth to the bank for them.

When Bob's mind started to go and he couldn't be safely left alone, Betty again looked at having home care. To her amazement, the cost to have just one person in the house 24 hours 7 days a week was going to be more than if Bob lived in the nursing home! She and Bob had a nice nest egg, but they would be broke, and there would be nothing left for the kids in a couple of years if she had to pay for in-home care. To add insult to injury, the home care company had the nerve to say they would need to pay for two people whenever they needed to move Bob to give him a bath.

Betty hired the minimum help they could get by on, and their daughter, Sarah, spent many hours a week helping with house-keeping, cooking, and taking care of Bob. Sarah was now the only child that was consistently helping with the hands-on care of Bob. However, Sarah worried about the added strain being put on her already shaky marriage from being away from home so much and being exhausted all the time from working her regular job, maintaining her own house, and then helping her parents.

Knowing the sacrifice Sarah was making, Betty went to an attorney and had her will modified to leave Sarah some extra money once Betty and Melvin were both gone in recognition of the fact Sarah had sacrificed more than the other children. Even though Sarah had never asked, Betty thought it was the right thing to do and told Sarah what she had done. Although Sarah let her mom know it wasn't necessary to give her more than the other children, she was deeply moved and appreciative.

When Bob became incontinent and started falling when he tried to get out of bed on his own, they decided they had no choice but to move him to the nursing home. The nursing home told Betty she needed to "spend down" their assets, as they had too much to qualify for any help for Bob. The nursing home said Betty could stay in the house and keep her car and household furnishings but would need to spend down about half the remaining assets. Betty was also told she should take Bob's name off of everything. When she tried to take the house out of Bob's name, she found she could not, as she had no legal authority to sign Bob's name even though she was his wife. Betty found out that if she ever wanted to sell the house, she would have to have a "guardianship" set up for Bob, and it would be expensive and time consuming, and a judge would tell her how she was allowed to spend Bob's half of the money once the house sold and that, most likely, the judge would require Bob's money to be paid to the nursing home. Betty felt good that she was at least able to set up the bank accounts so Bob's name was no longer on them.

At the huge amount the nursing home cost per year, it didn't take long before the Hoppers had spent down half their Medicaid countable assets and Bob was on Medicaid. Every time Betty went to see him, he asked to come home, and he hated the roommate he had been forced to take as the government benefits only paid for a shared room. As Bob didn't remember why he was in the nursing home, this conversation was repeated every time he saw Betty.

Shortly after Bob was placed on Medicaid, Betty had a heart attack and passed away. Myrtle attended Betty's funeral. Myrtle was surprised at the extravagant funeral Betty had, as it seemed very unlike her. She also noticed that none of Betty's favorite songs were sung, and she wasn't dressed in the outfit she always told Myrtle she wanted to be dressed in when she passed. Of course, Myrtle had no way of knowing that Betty had never told her children what kind of funeral she wanted.

Soon after Betty's passing, the children learned that the house was now owned by Bob, as Bob and Betty had owned it under a joint and survivor deed. They also found out that since Bob was on Medicaid, Medicaid might make them sell the house or put a lien on it and take it after Bob passed away.

When the children met with the probate attorney, they found out that Betty's will left everything to Bob. Betty had always assumed she would pass away after Bob and never thought about what might happen if she passed first. As she had not gone to an elder law attorney, the attorney had never brought up strategies to preserve their assets in case Betty passed before Bob. Even though the will left everything to Bob since he outlived Betty, some of the children were also upset because they saw Sarah was supposed to get more money than the rest if Bob had already passed away. One sister started loudly "whispering" that Sarah must have made Betty change her will to favor her.

As the family talked with the attorney about the will, the attorney surprised them when she told them that basically none of the assets would go through the will. Not only did the house pass outside of the will, but the children now found out that all the bank accounts passed outside of the will as well. Although Betty never knew her bank accounts wouldn't go through her will, the consequence of naming Frank to all the accounts so he could help with the banking was that once Betty passed, Frank became the owner of the accounts because they had been set up as joint and survivor.

When the children objected and said they knew their parents wanted all their assets divided between all of the kids like the will said, Frank was initially quiet. He then said he would need to think about what was fair.

Frank later told his siblings that it wouldn't have made any sense for the bank accounts to go through the will, as then the accounts would have just gone to their dad and been spent at the nursing home. Frank said, after thinking about it further, his parents must have wanted him to receive the bank accounts because he had helped them with paying their bills and making deposits. When Sarah told Frank their parents never intended for Frank to get the bank accounts, Frank became angry and told Sarah and the other siblings they were always taking advantage of Mom and Dad when they received gifts and loans they didn't pay back and that he was the only responsible one in the family who never took a dime from their parents, and therefore, he was keeping the bank accounts.

Frank and his wife went on a cruise and bought new vehicles. Frank and Sarah and their siblings stopped talking to each other. Sarah and her husband separated, with Sarah's husband telling her she had allowed her family to take advantage of her.

Shortly after coming back from vacation, Frank received a notice that Medicaid was going to terminate Bob's Medicaid and impose a penalty because the bank accounts, in Medicaid's opinion, should have been left by Betty to Bob. When Frank asked the nursing home what would happen, he was told that Medicaid was going to impose a lengthy penalty during which time Medicaid wouldn't pay for Bob's nursing home bill. The nursing home went on to tell Frank that unless he or someone paid the nursing home, Bob would need to leave.

When Myrtle Antt heard about all the problems the Hopper family was having, she felt incredibly sad and at the same time, very grateful that she and Melvin had taken the time to start planning for all the things that might happen in later life years before and had involved their children to the extent necessary so they understood and could follow the plan.

Weren't the Antts smart and the Hoppers foolish? Well…even with a good plan that is frequently updated like the Antts, everything may not go so smoothly, and even with no plan, things may not go as horrible as they did for the Hoppers. However, with proper thought and planning, the odds certainly increase that things will go your way and make life much smoother and peaceful for all involved.

However, without thinking about your goals, desires, and possible problems that may arise, you can't make a plan. Once you have thought about your goals, unless you create a plan, you are as unlikely to achieve your goals as you are to drive to a new destination by just jumping in your car and leaving without consulting a map, directions, or GPS!

We have found that failure to develop and periodically update a well-thought-out senior estate plan is costly, financially as well as emotionally.

Let's look at some of the places where the Hopper's failed to plan.

§ 2.2.
FAILURE TO HAVE EVEN A BASIC ESTATE PLAN

Like many people, the Hoppers didn't think they needed an "estate plan." Everyone needs a plan that clearly and legally provides for where your assets go when you pass away. In fact, most people understand the need for at least a last will and testament even if they haven't put one in place yet. However, it is just as important to have the proper legal documents in place, authorizing someone to make financial and health-care decisions for you when you can't make those decisions yourself. Further, you need to make sure you name the right people to make those decisions. Some children are good with money and finances, but may not be able to make difficult health-care decisions in a time of crisis.

If a person becomes incapacitated, and beforehand never put a plan in place to legally name someone to make health-care and financial decisions through properly created power-of-attorney documents, then the family will have to go to probate court, have the incapacitated person declared incompetent, and have a guardianship established. After that, the judge who oversees the guardianship will be involved in any decisions affecting the incapacitated person.

Sometimes children fight with one another on who should be the guardian. Often an incapacitated parent who is put through a guardianship hearing will have hard feelings against the children. Even a person who is not legally competent may still resent being officially declared incompetent.

In the Hoppers' case, the fact that Bob had no financial power of attorney allowing Betty to act on his behalf prevented her from being able to put the house into her name, and it prevented her from later being able to sell the house unless she went to court and became Bob's guardian and got a judge's permission to sell the house.

§ 2.3.
FAILURE TO UNDERSTAND HOW THE PARTS OF YOUR ESTATE PLAN FIT TOGETHER

When Medicaid told Betty to get assets out of Bob's name, she was happy she was able to set the bank accounts up so they were just in her and Frank's names. Someone had once told her and Bob it was good to add a trustworthy child to the bank accounts so the child could help do the banking. Never once did it dawn on Betty that she had just made a major change to her estate plan. By adding Frank to her accounts, they would no longer pass through her will but instead, the accounts would be 100 percent owned by Frank when Betty passed away. Betty, like many people, mistakenly thought her will would somehow govern what happened to all of her assets.

Problems often occur because people don't realize how all parts of their estate plan fit together. In the Hopper's situation, if Bob had passed first, then Betty passed, Sarah still wouldn't have received the amount Betty intended, as the bank accounts were unintentionally set up to pass to Frank.

A senior estate planning attorney will take the time to discuss all of your assets, determine how those assets will pass upon death, and explain how all parts of your estate plan fit together so you don't unintentionally leave someone more or less than you intended.

§ 2.4.
FAILURE TO TAKE MEDICAID INTO ACCOUNT WHEN CREATING AN ESTATE PLAN

Betty never thought about what might happen to Bob and his Medicaid benefits if she passed first. She didn't realize how Medicaid might treat the house, and she didn't think about what might happen if Bob inherited assets from her through her will.

Further, no one told Betty that in addition to Frank becoming the owner of the bank accounts because of how they were set up, Medicaid would treat the accounts going to Frank as an improper transfer and impose a gift penalty upon Bob. The sad consequence of such an outcome leaves Bob in a terrible position at a time when he is unable to do anything to protect himself. Basically, Bob's Medicaid will be terminated, and the nursing home won't be paid during the penalty period. As a result, the nursing home will likely try to evict Bob for nonpayment.

A senior estate planning attorney would have brought these issues up and discussed strategies to achieve the best outcome.

§ 2.5.
FAILURE TO PLAN FUNERALS

Have you thought about what type of funeral you'd like? Even if you haven't spent much time thinking about it, you probably know whether you want to be cremated. You probably know whether you want a traditional service or something different. But...does anyone else know what you want? This is what happened to Betty. It is possible that she and Bob had talked over with each other what they wanted. But when Betty passed, Bob was no longer able to plan Betty's funeral, and he wasn't able to communicate her wishes to anyone else.

When children have to guess at what type of funeral you want, many things happen. First of all, you are unlikely to get the kind of funeral service you would have desired. Additionally, the funeral will likely cost much more than you would have paid. Since the children are also grieving at the time the funeral is planned, emotions can run strong and arguments can occur. Severe arguments can happen when children strongly disagree on funeral plans. This often happens where one child believes a parent wanted to be cremated and the other child is certain the parent was against cremation.

Funeral planning is something you can expect to discuss when dealing with a senior estate planning attorney.

§ 2.6.
FAILURE TO HAVE A MEANINGFUL PLAN TO AGE AT HOME

Like most people, the Hoppers and the Antts wanted to age at home. However, at some point the Antts realized in their conversations with their elder care attorney that their old home was impractical and wouldn't provide a safe or cost-effective place to live if they needed assistance. The Antts determined what they needed in a home, thought about decreasing their maintenance obligations and provided themselves a financial safety net to make sure things could be paid for if home care was needed.

On the other hand, the Hoppers didn't think about all the problems that might lurk in their current home. Features they might have loved when they were younger (such as large yards or multi-levels) became burdens. The Hoppers also had no plan on how care would be provided if it was ever needed. While some of the children helped out, it still wasn't enough to provide a peaceful and safe home for Bob and Betty. Further, no thought-out plan on how to compensate those children who helped out was ever put into place. In fact, the plan that Betty and Bob ultimately put in place tore the family apart when Betty passed.

§ 2.7.
CONCLUSION

As most of you probably recognized, the beginning of this chapter contained a takeoff on Aesop's fable of the ant and the grasshopper. As you may recall, many versions of the tale have an ant industriously working during the summer to put food away for the winter. Meanwhile the grasshopper scoffs at the ant for wasting those beautiful summer days. When winter comes, the ant is safe and snug and well fed, and the grasshopper goes hungry. Sometimes the fable ends with a saying such as "Beware of winter, before it comes."

The later years of life are but another season: a season the lucky among us get to experience. In order to increase the odds that the winter season of life is one that is happy and peaceful, it is necessary to prepare for winter by creating and maintaining a well-thought-out senior estate plan long before winter knocks on your door.

For more information, visit the website of

The Law Offices of Michael L. Brumbaugh Co., L.P.A.

at **www.brumbaughelderlaw.com**

"...AND TO MY FAVORITE AUTO
REPAIR SHOP OWNER,
I LEAVE...."

CHAPTER 3

SIX MISCONCEPTIONS ABOUT WILLS

Thorpe A. Facer, Esquire

§ 3.1.
INTRODUCTION

Ah, the wonderful and whacky world of wills! For a document that is so commonly known, so commonly referred to, and so commonly written about, there are an uncommon number of misconceptions about what a will is, how it works, and what it's supposed to do, not to mention why it's important. This chapter discusses six common misconceptions about wills with the hope that clearing up those misconceptions will lead to a better understanding of what a will is and why a properly drawn will, as part of a comprehensive estate and elder care plan, is important. For have no doubt, wills are critically important and a document every adult should have.

§ 3.2.
MISCONCEPTION NUMBER 1:
A WILL IS ALL I NEED

Have you ever seen the television commercial where the man in the ad tells you that for $79.99, you can order your own will—legal in all 50 states—and take back the law from the lawyers? The implication, of course, is that a will is all you need. Baloney. A will is only part of a complete and comprehensive plan.

In basic terms, a will is a document that tells your chosen representative (commonly called an executor) how to wind up your financial affairs and to whom to distribute your assets after your death. By its very nature, then, a will is only effective after death. What about all the years between making the will and death? How are your affairs handled if you become sick or disabled in some fashion? Your will, even if it's the best will ever written by the greatest attorney who ever lived, won't help you while you're alive.

In 1900, the life expectancy in this country was about 47 years. Now, life expectancy reaches, and for some groups of people, exceeds 78 years. Modern medicine works miracles keeping us alive longer. But this longevity can come with a price: alive but with a disability. Take, for example, an 87-year-old man. In the past decade, this gentleman has had two major shoulder surgeries (wanted to keep playing golf), beaten skin cancer (probably from exposure to the sun while playing golf), had a hip replaced (got to keep playing golf), and had a pacemaker put in. Fifty years ago, this man wouldn't have lived to see age 87. Now he's alive...but suffers from Alzheimer's disease. He must be taken care of in every aspect of his life. He is the living proof that an important question that must be answered as part of any estate and elder care plan is: What happens if I don't die but instead become sick?

Because a will only takes effect after death, it cannot answer this question. A will cannot give another person the authority to act on your behalf when you are unable to do so, because it doesn't take effect until you are dead. For this, you need comprehensive planning that includes powers of attorney and possibly one or more trusts. A will doesn't give end-of-life or living will instructions. A will doesn't coordinate who your beneficiaries should be on your life insurance policies or individual retirement accounts. Only a comprehensive plan, of which a will is an important part, will provide you with the planning you need to have peace of mind while you are alive and well, alive but disabled, and peace of mind for your loved ones after your death.

§ 3.3.
MISCONCEPTION NUMBER 2: A WILL TAKES CARE OF ALL OF MY ASSETS AND MONEY

The surviving members, except one, of Mr. Smith's (name changed) family were gathered in my conference room screaming at me and at each other because the family was not inheriting the bulk of Mr. Smith's assets. How could this be? Where was the life insurance money? Where were the hundreds of thousands of dollars from the IRAs? Despite my explanations, everybody left dissatisfied. Several legal challenges to the will followed resulting in thousands of dollars of fees and costs to the family. What happened?

The answer is summed up in one simple concept: probate versus nonprobate assets. A will only affects probate assets, which are assets that are part of the estate. Many assets that people have, everyday types of assets, are not part of the estate, and the will does not control them. An easy example is a life insurance policy, which is a contract between the insurance company and the owner/insured that upon the insured's death, the insurance company will pay the death benefits to whomever has been designated as the beneficiary of the policy. Unless the estate is designated as the beneficiary of the policy, the life insurance money is not controlled by the will. It passes outside of probate.

Another common example is a checking account. Many older people add the name of a son or daughter who lives close by to their checking account for ease of paying bills. What these people may not realize is that by adding another owner on the account, when the original owner dies, that account is not subject to probate and is not affected by the will. Why? Because an owner of the account, the adult child who was added for convenience, is still alive. Probate only affects those assets where there are no surviving owners. This concept explains why there is usually no probate when the first of a married couple dies. Most married couples own their assets jointly. When the first one passes away, no probate is required because an owner, the surviving spouse, is still alive.

Common examples of assets that don't pass through probate and aren't affected by the will:

- Individual retirement accounts and annuities. Again, just like the life insurance policy, the owner of the IRA or annuity will have designated a beneficiary to receive what's left upon the owner's death. The will doesn't touch this money.
- Accounts with a payable-on-death designation, such as a certificate of deposit (CD). Upon the owner's death, the CD is automatically paid to the designated beneficiary.
- Investments that are marked transfer on death. Similar to payable on death, a transfer-on-death designation transfers the investment immediately to the named beneficiary.
- Assets held in trust. The terms of the trust govern who receives the assets of the trust. The will has no effect.

Unknown to Mr. Smith's family, he had named his most recent lady friend as the beneficiary of his life insurance policies and his IRAs. His will, which distributed his probate assets equally to his children, didn't affect the life insurance or IRA one bit. And absent being able to prove fraud or undue influence of the lady friend over Mr. Smith, there was nothing the family could do. If you want to truly understand what your existing estate plan does and doesn't do, sit down with an attorney and determine which category your assets fall under: probate or nonprobate. Knowing this makes all the difference in the world.

§ 3.4.
MISCONCEPTION NUMBER 3: WILLS ARE AN EASY DO-IT-YOURSELF PROJECT

What could be simpler? Order one of those fill-in-the-blank will forms or purchase software to create your own will. Simple, right? Nope. Let's assume for a moment that you are looking at one of the fill-in-the-blank will forms; what do you put in the blanks? Your name, the name of your spouse, your children's names—good so far. What next? Name an executor, but what does an executor do, what qualifications should you be looking for? Do you look for physical proximity or financial acumen? The list of questions you need to answer is long, and the fill-in-the-blank form does not provide the counseling necessary to make the best possible decisions.

Here are just some of the issues that need to be addressed when considering a will:

1) What happens if one of your beneficiaries dies before you?
2) For married couples, how do you avoid the common trap of leaving everything to each other when one spouse is or might be in the nursing home?
3) Are there tax issues that the will should address?
4) Are there step-up in tax basis issues on some of the assets?
5) If all your beneficiaries were to predecease you, who would your "ultimate" beneficiary be?

6) Do any children or grandchildren have special needs? How should those needs be addressed in the will?

7) Are there any family issues such as shaky marriages, spendthrift beneficiaries, family members who don't get along, and/or addiction issues?

8) Is a second marriage or a blended family involved? How do you protect both sides of the family while being fair to all? Do both sides of the family get along? Should you name coexecutors, with one from each side? These issues are among the most serious and difficult, especially if not addressed properly from the beginning.

9) Is a civil union involved? How should that be handled?

10) Who should be named as executor? Should there be coexecutors? Alternates?

11) Are there items that need to be left to specific individuals? Should anyone receive a right of first refusal to purchase something such as business assets?

12) Is there a family business involved? If less than all of the beneficiaries are involved in the business, how do you treat everyone fairly without destroying the ability of those who are involved to continue running the business while ensuring those not involved receive a fair inheritance?

As noted above, these are only some of the counseling issues and decisions that need to be addressed when making a will. And as is clear from the discussion of Misconception Number 1 (A will is all I need), these issues don't even touch on the bigger picture of planning not only for after death, but for life and making the most of it. A will is definitely not an easy do-it-yourself project.

§ 3.5.
MISCONCEPTION NUMBER 4: IF I HAVE A WILL, MY ESTATE DOES NOT GO THROUGH PROBATE COURT

A will is actually an admission ticket to probate court! If you have a will, and if you have probate assets (remember the important distinction between probate and nonprobate assets), your estate most likely will have to go through probate court. As an aside, I say "most likely" because some states have expedited noncourt processes for very small estates; these alternate processes avoid a formal probate. Consult with your local elder care and estate planning attorney to learn more.

What is probate? The concept is quite simple. If you own a checking account in your name only, the bank will freeze the funds in that account upon your death. When do the funds get released? When the bank receives the appropriate authorization from a probate court. Probate, therefore, is the process of verifying the validity of the will (if there is one), then overseeing a decedent's estate to ensure all the assets are gathered, final bills paid, and distribution according to the terms of the will properly made. Probate court can be short or long, simple or complex, relatively inexpensive or costing thousands and thousands of dollars. Much depends on what the assets are, how they are titled, how easy they are to locate, the number of claims against the estate, and whether there are other issues, such as family disputes, involved.

Is probate always "bad?" No. In some circumstances probate is advisable. Some examples include when there are numerous claims or potential claims against the estate. Judicial oversight can make handling those claims a more orderly and (sometimes) easier process. Another example is when there are family disputes and potential challenges to the validity of the will. Again, having an impartial judge keeping an eye on things not only keeps the process moving but also provides a structured framework within which the parties, using court rules and procedures, can resolve the disputes.

Should you avoid probate? In many cases, yes. Several reasons make avoiding probate a good idea. First, probate can be time consuming and expensive. I've seen various numbers bandied about, but most studies indicate that probate takes an average of at least fifteen months. For a family business or farm, having assets tied up for that length of time can spell disaster. Expense is also a consideration. As indicated above, the actual cost of probating a particular estate depends on many factors, but every estate, simple or complex, requires a certain amount of paperwork, court appearances, notice published in the newspaper, and so on. One study suggests that the average cost of probate is between five and ten percent of the value of the estate. While not all costs associated with dealing with the assets of a decedent can be avoided, many can with proper planning that will allow your estate to avoid going through probate.

Second, probate is an open process. Anyone who knows your name can go to the courthouse and look at your will, the inventory of your assets, your debts, and claims against your estate. I have heard of a small town newspaper which, until recently, published the will and inventory of assets of each town member who died! Probably good for that paper's circulation figures but a real loss of privacy for the family. Avoiding probate preserves your privacy.

Third, as alluded to above, planning to avoid probate means that you have more thoroughly planned for not only after death but for the rest of your life come what may. Doing comprehensive planning is the best way to avoid probate, but such planning has the more important benefit of solving many problems before they begin. For those problems that can't be avoided, such as illness or loss of mental capacity, planning allows for simpler and better resolutions.

§ 3.6.
MISCONCEPTION NUMBER 5: I DON'T NEED A WILL AT ALL

"Why bother with a will? Everyone knows the government will take it all anyway," so commented a person attending one of my recent seminars. Is this person right? Of course not. With the tax laws in effect at the time of writing this chapter, neither the state nor the federal government "takes" anything from over 98 percent of all estates. So why bother? Because you want to make sure your loved ones are protected and your wishes followed. Having a will is a first step in that direction.

Every state has rules and laws about what happens when a person dies without a will. These are known as the laws of intestacy. Examining each state's laws of intestacy is beyond the scope of this chapter. What is more important, however, is this: while each state has rules and laws, each state also says that any individual can make his or her own rules about how his or her estate will be handled so long as the rules are properly drafted! This means each of one of us has the opportunity to ensure that our estate is handled exactly the way we want it to be handled and not according to the rules set forth by a state legislature that knows nothing about our needs, our desires, and our unique circumstances.

What does properly drafted mean? To write your own rules, you need to put them in writing and have them witnessed according to the requirements of the state where you live. For most states, that means your signature has to be witnessed by at least two people who are not related to you and who are not beneficiaries of your estate. Some states add the requirement that the signatures be notarized. Also, your own rules have to comply with the requirements of the law in that you can't make a rule that would cause someone else to violate a law such as the tax code.

So how do you do this? You make a will. You do comprehensive estate and elder care planning. You address all the issues so that your estate is handled just the way you want. Here are some examples of what can happen when a person dies without a will.

A typical law of intestacy requires that when a married person dies without a will, one-half of the estate goes to the surviving spouse and one-half goes to the decedent's children. Such an outcome can have devastating results for the surviving spouse who likely needs all of the assets to survive and live with any quality of life. The surviving spouse will be left with diminished income (50 percent or less of the deceased spouse's pension and the loss of the smaller of the two Social Security checks) and only one-half of the assets. This is not the way to ensure your spouse's quality of life.

Same scenario as above, but this time there is a blended family with each spouse having children from prior relationships. In many blended families, particularly those later in life, one spouse wants to ensure that the other is taken care of, but also wants to ensure that all of his or her assets go to his or her children. However, dying without a will makes that division of assets impossible. First, as noted above, the surviving spouse receives only one-half of the deceased spouse's assets. The deceased spouse's children receive one-half, but that's all they get. The other half goes to the children of the surviving spouse after he or she dies. How much better it would be, for the surviving spouse and the deceased spouse's children, if the deceased spouse had planned using a will and other tools such as a trust. Such a plan would have provided for the surviving spouse while also ensuring that the children of the deceased spouse received everything left upon the death of the surviving spouse.

Similar situations, all sharing the commonality of an undesired outcome, exist in great numbers. Planning solves these problems by preventing them before they happen.

§ 3.7.
MISCONCEPTION NUMBER 6: THERE WILL BE A FORMAL READING OF MY WILL

What a tense moment! The entire family and beneficiaries gathered around the conference room table with the lawyer (always a distinguished-looking older gentleman) solemnly taking the will out of the envelope and reading it out loud. As the will is read, various family members cry out with delight, gasp in shock or disgust, cast evil looks at others around the table, flash little smiles of content or antagonistic delight. Loud complaints are heard and threats are made as the will reading comes to its conclusion. The stage is set for conflict and perhaps violence.

We've all seen these scenes in the movies or on television, or we've read them in books. Do formal readings of the will happen in real life? The answer is no. No state requires a formal reading of the will. So why do we see them in movies or read them in books? Because a formal reading of the will is a wonderful plot device to bring all the antagonists together and set the stage for the conflict, which will form the basis for the rest of the movie or book. Authors and script writers learned long ago that there is no better or quicker way to introduce the characters and set up the rest of the story.

Formal readings of a will are permitted and can be beneficial in that confusion can be reduced as all the heirs and beneficiaries know what is going on even if they don't agree with it. If there are issues, a formal reading can get them out in the open, usually the first step in resolving them. But with families being more geographically widespread than ever before, it is difficult getting everyone together except, perhaps, at the funeral. And that's not a good time to be doing anything other than grieving and offering comfort to loved ones.

The question then becomes, how do people find out what's in a will? Again, we return to the probate process, which requires that each person named as a beneficiary of a will, or who is an heir of the deceased, be notified of the death and provided with a copy of the will. Throughout the probate process, court rules require accountings to the heirs and beneficiaries so they are kept informed of what is going on. And before the probate can be ended and closed out, each beneficiary is required to either give written consent to how the estate has been handled or is given the opportunity to go into court and voice objections to the probate judge, who then rules on the validity of the objections.

§ 3.8.
CONCLUSION

Sometimes people call my office and say, "I just want a simple will." After nearly 25 years of practicing law, I still don't know what a simple will is. I've seen wills that were short but not particularly simple. I've seen family situations that were straightforward yet still not simple. And I've seen the complex. People don't want a simple will; they want a will that works. More importantly, they want a plan that works. To have such a plan, visit your local elder care and senior estate planning attorney.

For more information, visit

Thorpe Facer on his website

at **www.facerlawoffice.com**

THE JOURNEY OF LIFE OFFERS
MANY CHOICES!

CHAPTER 4

LIFE CARE PLANNING

J. Randall Clinkscales,
Kansas elder law attorney

§ 4.1
INTRODUCTION

Life care planning is a holistic approach to assisting families facing issues of aging, chronic illness, or disability. It goes beyond the traditional transactional approach to delivery of legal services to families. The typical life care planning law firm establishes a relationship with the family so that services (including the preparation of appropriate legal documents, advance care planning, care coordination, benefits coordination, coordination of planning with other professionals, maintenance of independence, and end-of-life planning) are all considered in developing an individualized life care plan.

Our firm, Clinkscales Elder Law Practice, P.A., has specialized in life care planning since 2006. Through life care planning we are given the opportunity to help our clients through difficult times, acting as their guide through the complexities of aging, chronic illness, or disability. Life care planning provides the client with individualized answers and a road map for successful case-by-case outcomes. The typical transactional approach to legal services simply does not provide a method for addressing the complex issues of aging.

§ 4.2.
OVERRIDING GOAL OF THE ELDERLY AND THOSE WHO HAVE CHRONIC ILLNESSES

I began my journey into elder law and eventually into life care planning as a result of a family experience. In 2001, I became the caregiver for my grandmother. When I began my journey with her, the doctors gave me the prognosis, "Your grandmother has three to six months to live." My grandmother ended up having three to six months to live for the next ten years! My experiences with her transformed my law practice and how I work with my clients.

I conduct workshops for seniors and those who have chronic illnesses, as well as for healthcare professionals trying to help those families. When I ask seniors what their number-one goal is when it comes to the remainder of their lives, the answer is invariably "to live at home as long as possible." That was the same goal that my grandmother shared with me.

This response is contrary to what many believe that seniors or chronically ill people want, which is to get on Medicaid or other government programs. The "millionaire on Medicaid" is an aberration, if not a myth. Instead, the senior will say that, if given an opportunity, the first choice would be to stay at home, to keep control, and to maintain dignity. If it is the goal of the elderly and chronically ill to stay at home as long as possible, how do they develop a plan so that can happen? And who can set up and monitor that plan? The question really becomes "How does the elderly person find, get, and pay for appropriate care to stay independent for as long as possible?"

Obviously, the elderly and chronically ill person's health and abilities will change over time. Even so, it does not mean we have to give up on that person's goal to stay independent. Even if the person's own home exposes that person to too great a risk and there is a need to move to another environment (such as independent living, assisted living, or even a nursing home), we still want that person to get good care and maintain independence, as well as dignity.

In caring for my grandmother, we were able to maintain her in her home for six years. During that process, she actually went into hospice care on two different occasions. (A Medicare-funded hospice program is generally available to people who have a prognosis of not living more than six months.)

After six years, I made the tough decision to move my grandmother from Fort Worth, Texas, to be near my home in Kansas. I moved my 92-year-old, 90-pound, emaciated grandmother into an assisted living facility. Guess what happened? She actually blossomed. Once she started getting good care, her life improved. The transition to assisted living was not completely smooth. As I will explain later, there were some bumps and bruises along the way.

§ 4.3.
HEALTH-CARE DILEMMA

If I am sick and I go to the doctor, the doctor may spend some time with me and will typically give me some medication and send me on my way. When I get home, my wife will ask me, "What did the doctor say?" My answer is rarely satisfactory to her. Frankly, when I am sick, I do not listen well. I just want to get better, and I will take whatever medicine the doctor gives me.

There are two problems with the current delivery of medical services. First, the health-care provider is assuming that he or she is dealing with a well-informed, enabled consumer who can take the advice of the health-care provider and put it to work. Many times that is not realistic. It is often the case that we end up with multiple visits to a health-care professional, usually precipitated by a crisis situation. The chronic illness is not managed, and recovery is delayed or not even accomplished. Second, it is an example of a reactive-type approach. The senior went to the doctor when he was sick. Rather, he should go to the health-care provider so that he can stay well. Compounding the problem is that many times multiple health-care providers are needed to manage a variety of medical issues, yet communication and coordination is fragmented or nonexistent among providers.

When I moved my grandmother from Texas to Kansas, she was in a health maintenance organization (HMO) program. I discovered that even though she was in a HMO program, she had different health-care providers providing different medications without consulting each other. In addition, her health-care providers never sat back and looked at her medications to see which ones were necessary and which ones were not, and whether the various medications had interactions with each other, which could be problematic.

After I moved my grandmother to Kansas, I took her to my family doctor, and we went through her medications. Our care coordinator (more on that later) became involved. She spent time visiting with my grandmother, found out what her habits were, and found out when during the day she felt better than other times. We discovered that a lot of her weight loss was due to medications that upset her stomach, resulting in her not eating sufficiently.

By working with our care coordinator and my grandmother's new doctor, we were able to change the timing of medications and even eliminate many medications. The result was that my grandmother went from 14 different daily medications to four medications. Her appetite increased, and she gained weight back to her normal 130 pounds.

§ 4.4.
ESTATE PLANNING APPROACH

In the typical estate planning approach, potential clients fill out a questionnaire about their assets and their liabilities. They fill out a sheet that explains to the attorney to whom they want their property to go and even whom they want to act on their behalf if they lose capacity. In a more thorough estate plan, there will even be discussions about various insurance products and perhaps taxes.

The typical estate plan is a plan that focuses on dying, not a plan that focuses on living a long time. After creating and signing the estate plan, it is put away and is probably not pulled out again until death or incapacity. Other family members may not even be aware of the estate plan, or their role in it.

§ 4.5.
TRADITIONAL ELDER LAW APPROACH

The term *elder law* is fairly new. In fact, even today, if I tell someone that I am an elder law attorney, they look quizzically at me. The typical scenario for an elder law attorney arises when a family's loved one goes into a nursing home or develops a chronic illness that requires care that cannot necessarily be provided by the family. The family contacts an elder law attorney.

The traditional approach to elder law is crisis based. That means the client is in a crisis, and the planning is going to focus on asset preservation and/or government benefit qualification. Typically, the children, or even the spouse, are panicked about how to pay for care, how to prevent losing all of the assets, and how to keep something for the family.

I understand. That is the family's most immediate concern. As they say, "That is where the bleeding is." In asset-focused planning, assets typically are going to be "sheltered" from long-term-care costs. That may mean gifting away assets to a family member; it may involve shifting assets from one spouse to the other; or it may mean special types of trusts.

The traditional elder law approach is to set up a plan to qualify a chronically ill person for Medicaid or some other government benefit. It is going to involve the impoverishment of the chronically ill person. That is not necessarily a bad thing, but is that always the best thing for the client? Once the Medicaid plan is developed for the client, that elder law attorney's job is "done." The family understands that if they need additional services, they will need to re-engage (rehire) the elder law attorney.

Back to my grandmother: My grandmother was in assisted living. As a general rule, the cost of assisted living is not going to be paid for by Medicaid. From a financial standpoint, it would have made a lot more sense to put my grandmother into a nursing home and let Medicaid pay for her care. We would have been able to preserve assets for her and eventually for the family. However, she really was flourishing in the assisted living facility. She liked being there. Consequently, under the life care plan approach, it was better to utilize her resources to help her stay in the assisted living facility for as long as possible, even if that meant spending more of her assets than we would have had to under a nursing home scenario using Medicaid.

§ 4.6.
CAREGIVER DILEMMA

One dilemma that sometimes gets overlooked by the general public is the role of the caregiver. When we have a person who is elderly or who has a chronic illness or disability, typically, one if not several people are going to be involved in the care giving. In 2012 more than 15 million Americans provided unpaid care valued at more than $216 billion for persons who have Alzheimer's and other dementias, while actual payments for health care for those who have Alzheimer's disease and other dementias are estimated at $203 billion for 2013[1]. So, more than half of the "cost" of care is donated caregiver services. Even more frightening is the impact on the finances and health of caregivers.

As a caregiver for my grandmother, I woke up some mornings feeling as if I were drowning. I did not know what to do next. I did not know where to go for assistance. I did not know how to access services. I was faced with multiple choices about what type of care my grandmother should be receiving, where she should be living, whether I should be opting out of certain health-care programs and accessing others that could better help her.

Some of the families I work with have sat in my office, crying from exhaustion or frustration. Caregiver stress continues even after a loved one enters a nursing home or is given other institutional care. Almost no caregiver knows or understands the full extent of a nursing home's obligation to a patient, yet the caregiver is expected to oversee the loved one's care. The caregiver becomes the eyes, ears, nose, and feelings of the loved one. The obligations as a caregiver do not suddenly go away just because the loved one has been placed in the nursing home. In many ways, the role becomes more complex.

Caregiver burnout is a huge dilemma that should not be over-looked. The typical crisis-based elder law practice is not equipped to handle or face that type of problem, other than to perhaps refer the caregiver to the appropriate agency. Again, with the traditional elder law service, the elder law attorney may not even be involved with the family when the caregiver burnout starts.

§ 4.7.
LIFE CARE PLANNING APPROACH

Lawyers who have elderly and chronically ill clients have seen the dilemmas described above. When I was trying to help my grandmother, I saw that there were so many questions that were beyond my capabilities to answer, as a lawyer. As a result, my firm evolved into a life care planning firm. We belong to the Life Care Planning Law Firms Association, and we are one of the original members of that organization. (It is not necessary to belong to that organization to provide the services that I am going to describe below.)

Because so much of my planning for my grandmother dealt with her goal to stay at home or to stay as independent as possible, and to stay healthy and be involved in all of the decision-making, we brought a person into my office whom we call a care coordinator. Under the life care planning model, the care coordinator can be anyone from a social worker with some geriatric training to a registered nurse. We currently have three different care coordinators who vary in their education and work backgrounds: One worked in a nursing home for over 14 years as a director; one is a licensed practical nurse, who also worked as a nursing home director for seven years; and one is a retired naturopathic physician. They all have one common thread: They all have worked with seniors and those who have chronic illnesses and disabilities. They know what good care looks like.

I do not want that point to pass: The care coordinators know what good care looks like and how to find it. When I was taking care of my grandmother and she was living at home, I had no idea what types of services were available, particularly for someone with limited financial resources. Please understand that my grandmother was living in Fort Worth, Texas, where you would think there would be a plethora of resources. However, I found the experience to be terribly frustrating. I tried solutions from as simple as having relatives check on her to meal deliveries, to senior companions and even hospice care, but never found a great solution. That is an understatement. I never even found an average solution.

Even after I moved my grandmother to assisted living in Kansas, I had no idea what types of services were appropriate and what my expectations should be. Should I expect someone to be in her room at all times so that she would never fall? Should I expect that no one would bother her and she would have all of the privacy in the world? When the doctor wanted to perform more tests on my grandmother, were those tests necessary, given my grandmother's condition, age, and goals? Was the additional medication that the doctor wanted to administer to my grandmother appropriate, given her age and health condition? Did I want to make the decision that my grandmother was not to be resuscitated should she go into cardiac arrest? When would that decision be appropriate?

These are common questions, and so many times families try to go at it alone.

With care coordinators and with a firm devoted to life care planning, this is what is going to happen:

- The family hires a life care planning law firm. Rather than a transaction, there is a relationship established between the law firm and its staff and the client and his or her family.
- Family involvement in the process becomes very important. At least some family members may be the caregivers and

will be working directly with the life care planning law firm.

- The legal staff and the care coordinator are going to spend time with the client and the client's spouse (if any), as well as the client's family. The care coordinator and legal staff are going to find out what quality of life the client wants, what the client's goals and aspirations are regarding health care, asset management and preservation, and end-of-life decisions.

- Certain staff members are assigned to a team for that client. The team will include the care coordinator, an attorney, a benefits specialist (with extensive background in Medicare, Medicaid, Social Security, and insurance), a veterans benefits specialist (if the client or the client's spouse is a veteran), as well as a paralegal who will assist in transfers of property and beneficiary designations.

- The care coordinator then visits with the client in the client's own environment. That environment may be the client's home or some other setting (such as independent living, assisted living, or a nursing home). As part of that assessment process, the care coordinator will obtain records regarding the health history of the client, including current medications and the purpose of those medications. The care coordinator will also assess the living environment: Is it appropriate for that client? Are modifications needed to make the living environment safer or more accommodating for that client? The assessment will also identify risks in that environment.

- The care coordinator then prepares an assessment report. That assessment report is provided to the life care planning team. The team evaluates the assessment, as well as the various assets and resources of the family. The team may also consult with the family's accountant, insurance professional, and investment advisor. The care coordinator may also consult with a health-care professional dealing with the client, as well as the caregivers, to ascertain their concerns. The care coordinator will make available to the life care planning team information about types of care resources that are available where that client lives. (Many of my clients live in rural areas where care or health resources may be more limited.)

- A meeting is then set up with the client and the family again. At that meeting, the report and recommendation from the life care planning team is reviewed with the client and the family. Decisions are made by the client and the family. A plan is then put into place.

- The plan will be multifaceted. It will make recommendations based on the client's care needs (sometimes the client is quite healthy and his or her care needs are being met. The care assessment, however, creates a baseline for the family). The plan may also include accessing benefits available in the client's area. It may be as simple as setting up a system for family and friends to call the client, meal delivery, or an emergency calling system, but it could include recommendations for 24-hour care or even for moving the client to a more secure environment. The plan may include a totally different approach to be taken to the estate planning documents. The estate planning documents are going to be more focused on how to access resources to take care of the client, though there may be an element of asset preservation, based on the desires of the client. Certain documents, such as a living will, power of attorney for financial decisions, and power of attorney for health-care decisions are going to be modified to more closely reflect the desires of the client in light of his or her particular circumstances. The planning process will also build in contingencies, so that if at some point additional nonprivate resources are needed, they can be accessed without any type of penalty (such as Medicaid, veterans' benefits, and the like). If public benefits are needed immediately, the plan will guide the client through that process.

- Life care planning does not stop there. The life care planning law firm continues to work with the family. The team assigned to the family meets regularly to review changes in health, laws, and available benefits. In a typical life care plan, the efforts continue for the rest of the client's lifetime (based on the terms of the agreement between the client and the law firm).

- The care coordinator helps the family coordinate care for the client who has a chronic illness. That may mean just monitoring the progress of the chronic illness with the family; it may mean bringing in outside care; or it may mean progressing to a different level of care.

- The care coordinator may make occasional visits to the client and provide reports to the family. The care coordinator will also answer questions for the family about whether their loved one is getting appropriate care, even if in an institutional setting. The care coordinator is going to know the standards imposed on appropriate care, and if the care the client is receiving falls short, the care coordinator will advise the family on how to improve their loved one's care and what avenues are available to improve that care.

- Under the life care plan, the financial and legal documents are continually evaluated and changed, based on the changing circumstances of the client or changes in the various laws and regulations that could adversely affect the client.

- The client's situation is continually evaluated to see what other benefits might be available to the client and the client's family. While, initially, Medicaid may not be necessary, the plan may evolve so that Medicaid becomes a more realistic alternative. It might involve advocating for the client to extend Medicare to help pay for care. It may mean tapping into veteran benefits. It might be qualifying the client for particular types of housing that may be sensitive to income and resources. It can also involve accessing insurance products that will help the client stay at home longer without the necessity of public benefits. The client's goals are continually reevaluated, based on his or her ever-evolving circumstances.

- In our firm, our life care plans are set up in such a fashion that the client has free access to our office and its resources without any additional charges. In our typical life care plans, the firm charges a substantial up-front fee and then an annual maintenance fee for as long as the firm and the client want to continue. Frankly, almost all our clients continue for the remainder of their lifetimes.

In my opinion, one of the most important parts of the life care plan comes near the end of the client's life. During the last 50 days or so of my grandmother's life, she moved to a nursing home. Her health really began to fail as she grew older. She was now 96 years of age. The care coordinator from my office worked with me and my grandmother in making some hard decisions at the end. My care coordinator gave me and my grandmother "permission" to do certain things and to refuse to do others. The care coordinator prepared both of us for the journey to the end.

When my grandmother passed away at age 96, I had real peace of mind that she was ready to go and was going out on her terms, as she had expressed them to me and the care coordinator. While I certainly miss her, I feel fortunate that I could be highly involved in the last 10 years of her life. I really could not have done it without the help of my care coordinator and the life care plan team.

When a family retains my office for a life care plan, they express tremendous relief. So many times a family has told me how much better they felt after hiring my firm, but more especially, after their loved one has passed away, universal gratitude is expressed to my office staff for the job they did for the family.

If your family is dealing with aging issues, chronic illness, or disabilities, life care planning is the complete guide you need for your journey.

If you would like more information about life care planning, go to **www.lcplfa.org** or visit the website of **Clinkscales Elder Law Practice, P.A.** at **www.clinkscaleslaw.com**

---

[1] Alzheimer's Association, 2013 Alzheimer's Disease Facts and Figures, http://www.alz. org/downloads/facts_figures_2013.pdf

I MADE HER PROMISE TO
TAKE CARE OF ME WHEN I'M OLDER
IF I BOUGHT HER A CELL PHONE NOW!

CHAPTER 5

FAMILY CAREGIVER AGREEMENTS

Fiona Van Dyck, Esquire

§ 5.1.
INTRODUCTION

Sophia had grown up in a loving, multigenerational home where she lived with her parents, her brother, and her maternal grandmother. When she would come home from school, her grandmother was always waiting for her with a hug, a kiss, a glass of milk, and a homemade snack. Sophia's favorite was the bread that her grandmother would bake and which would still be warm as she came through the door. She would smother the bread with butter and strawberry jam. This is how Sophia remembers her childhood—full of love, family, and freshly baked bread. As her grandmother aged and needed assistance, Sophia's mother, Grace, was there to care for her. As Grace would always say, "We take care of our own."

Sophia knew that when the time came, she would be there to care for her parents in the same way. After Sophia's father died, Grace continued to live in the house where Sophia had grown up and continued to be active in her community. Over time, however, it became apparent that Grace was beginning to have memory difficulties, and it became more difficult for her to manage in her home alone. It was decided that Grace would move into Sophia's home and join Sophia, her husband, and Sophia's two young sons. Grace sold her home and put the proceeds into a savings account at her local bank. Sophia refused to touch the money in Grace's bank account, and Grace liked the idea that she had something "just in case." And if "just in case" never occurred, then she had something to leave to her children to remember her by.

Over time, Grace's care needs increased to the point where Sophia needed to leave her job as a teaching assistant at the local elementary school to care for Grace. Of course, with an additional person living in the home and without Sophia's paycheck, the family had to cut back on expenses. And so, the "extra" things, such as Saturday family night out at the movies, Sophia's gym membership, and the boys' martial arts lessons, had to go.

One day, Grace slipped, fell, and broke her hip. Because of the break, Grace became wheelchair bound and completely dependent on Sophia for all of her needs. As Sophia's house was not equipped for a wheelchair, the family faced a dilemma. Do they bring in a contractor to reconfigure the house to accommodate the wheelchair or begin to look for another housing option for Grace?

Given Grace's care needs and the costs and the amount of time involved to make the house wheelchair friendly, Sophia and her husband decided that a nursing home would best be able to meet Grace's needs. Fortunately, they found one close to their home that had wonderful reviews from a friend whose father lived there. There was a room available for Grace but at a cost of nearly $10,000 per month. In eighteen months, Grace's entire nest egg had been used to pay her nursing home care costs.

It was at that point that a Medicaid application was made on Grace's behalf to pay for her long-term health-care needs. And yet, it did not need to be that way. Using a family caregiver agreement, Grace could have fairly paid Sophia, rather than the nursing home, for her care; Sophia's family's standard of living could have remain unchanged; and Grace could have been eligible to begin receiving Medicaid benefits much sooner.

§ 5.2.
THE ECONOMICS OF CAREGIVING

As a society, more and more of us are becoming caregivers for our parents and aging relatives. In fact, across the United States, there are over 61 million people providing unpaid care to their adult family members who are chronically ill, disabled, or elderly[2]. The value of the unpaid services that these family caregivers provide is estimated to be $450 billion per year. Consider this in comparison to the $203 billion that is being spent on paid homecare and nursing home services[3]. The amount of unpaid services is over twice as much! Every day for the next 19 years, 10,000 Americans will turn 65[4]. Given these statistics, the number of family caregivers will only continue to rise astronomically.

And who are these caregivers? Statistics show that approximately 66 percent of caregivers are women, and more than 37 percent of caregivers have children or grandchildren under the age of 18 living with them[5]. On average, caregivers are providing 20 hours per week of care for their loved ones; however, 13 percent of them are providing more than 40 hours per week of care[6]. Family caregivers are the bedrock that is allowing more and more people to remain safe and at home during their senior years. However, this care that is being freely provided does not come without a price. And that price is being paid by the caregivers themselves.

If you are providing 20 or more hours of care a week to loved one, is it possible to work more than a part-time job? Without a full-time job, what health benefits are being made available to these caregivers for themselves and their families? Hopefully, there is another individual, perhaps a spouse, in the family who is able to work and provide the necessary health benefits, but this is not always the case. Moreover, whenever one family member is taken out of the workforce, the effects are far reaching upon the entire family. Women who are family caregivers are two-and-a-half times more likely than noncaregivers to live in poverty and five times more likely to receive Supplemental Security Income (SSI)[7]. Families in which one member has a disability have lower incomes than families without members who have a disability[8]. And 47 percent of caregivers report that caregiving expenses caused them to use up *all* or *most* of their savings. The average family caregiver for someone age 50 or older spends approximately $5,500 per year on out-of-pocket caregiving expenses—more than 10 percent of the median income for a family caregiver[9].

Consider Sophia. After her mother came to live with her, Sophia found that she could no longer leave the home to work if she was going to care for her mother. This had a decided impact on her family's financial situation, regardless of whether she was the primary earner, and this is true for other family caregivers as well. Perhaps family vacations do not happen, perhaps children's college savings plans are not funded, and perhaps the family does not eat out as often. However minor the changes to a family's way of life may be without that other income, they are changes nonetheless that affect the family unit as a whole. Most family caregivers provide for their loved ones out of a sense of love and duty and without batting an eye to the sacrifices they are making.

As Sophia told me, this was her mother, and she would do whatever was needed for her for as long as she could. In Sophia's case, her mother had money that could have been used to pay for a home health worker or, indeed, for assisted living or nursing home care. Could that money have been used to pay Sophia for her role as her mother's caregiver and make up for Sophia's loss of income? The simple answer is yes. Sophia could have been paid for her services by way of a family caregiver agreement.

§ 5.3.
FAMILY CAREGIVER AGREEMENTS

A family caregiver agreement is essentially an employment contract between the caregiver and the care recipient. Many times the caregiver feels that she should not be paid for her services because she is doing it out of love. While it may be true that the caregiver is providing the services out of love, it does not change the fact that, economically, the caregiver is often in much worse financial shape because she is providing these services without pay. What the caregiver must come to realize is that she should not be financially penalized for taking care of her loved one. It is fair to be compensated, and it can also be a necessary tool in accessing government assistance to pay for long-term care costs when and if they become necessary. What the caregiver often does not take into consideration is the benefit that a caregiver agreement can provide to the family as a whole.

Family caregiver contracts must be able to stand up as a third party contract, that is, it must be as if the caregiver is someone unknown to the family, and the contract must be fair and reasonable considering all of the circumstances. For this and other reasons, it is incredibly important that the family caregiver agreement be drafted by an attorney with elder law or senior estate planning experience and take into consideration many factors, including those set forth below.

§ 5.3.1.
What Are the Care Needs?

One of the first factors that needs to be considered is what the care needs are, as this will help determine the fair market value of the services being provided. There are several types of services that the caregiver may be providing, including personal care services, skilled nursing services, geriatric care services, and financial management services. Each of these services has a different level of complexity and so a different level of compensation. Let's consider each one separately.

Personal care services include many of the things that a caregiver does on a daily basis. These include such things as assisting the care recipient with many of the activities of daily living such as eating, bathing, shaving, and toileting. This care is of the type that would be performed by a home health aide and does not require frequent medical or nursing judgment.

Conversely, skilled care services include such things as medication management, new diagnosis education, wound care, disease management, and post surgery care, to name a few. Even though the family caregiver may not have specific medical training in these regards, she is often called upon to perform these services.

Geriatric care services include many of the things that most caregivers are providing on a daily basis. These services include such things as finding appropriate solutions to problems before a crisis arises; monitoring medications to make sure there are no adverse reactions; coordinating medical appointments, providing transportation to them, and providing physicians with up to date information regarding the care recipient's status; advocating for the care recipient with his physicians and others; ensuring the care recipient is in a safe and disability friendly environment; providing personal counseling; and continually assessing the level of care needed. So often the family caregiver does all of these duties without giving them a single thought. However, there are individuals, usually with nursing or social work backgrounds and training, who make a career of providing these very services.

Finally, the caregiver is frequently called upon to act as the financial manager for the care recipient. This can include such things as monitoring investments, bank accounts, and credit cards. It can include making certain that the elderly care recipient is not being taken advantage of in some way or another. Unfortunately, the elderly are often "marks" for unscrupulous people, and without the benefit of a trusted family member or friend assisting them, they can lose their life savings.

In order to substantiate the need for the care that is being rendered, it is important to speak with the care recipient's physician about the care needs and the services that need to be provided. Ask the physician to provide a written report clearly stating that the services are needed for the care recipient's health and well-being. This is imperative if the care recipient will need Medicaid assistance, as it will prove to the Medicaid officials that the care was necessary and that it enabled the individual to remain at home for a period of time when they would otherwise have been forced to move to a care facility.

It is important to look at the care situation closely and determine the number of hours of care per week being provided and the level of that care. Once these are determined, local agencies that deliver such services can be contacted to determine the rates of pay. Only then can an assessment be made as to what is fair compensation based upon what one would pay a third party caregiver to provide those services. Doing this solidifies that the fee for the services is appropriate—again, something that will be important down the road if one needs the agreement to pass Medicaid's muster.

The family caregiver agreement should allow for the care recipient to have a say in the services the caregiver will provide. The family caregiver agreement can, and should, provide for such things as how often the care recipient will be taken shopping or to cultural activities. The care recipient should be able to personalize the agreement to take into consideration the things that she would like to do. Remember, this agreement is not just for the benefit of the caregiver but also for the benefit of the care recipient who is, after all, paying for the care.

§ 5.3.2.
It's a Job

The family caregiver agreement is really a contract for a job, and it should, therefore, include a job description. The caregiver's ability, willingness, and availability to do certain tasks should be assessed and addressed. The number of hours per week that the caretaker agrees to perform the caretaking tasks should be specified. Of course, provisions must be allowed for the potential for an increase in the number of hours needed, or conversely a decrease in the number of hours if the care recipient moves into assisted living or a nursing home.

The family caregiver agreement should also allow for the resignation of the caregiver and for the caregiver to assign duties to another. This is a contract without a predetermined end date, and circumstances may arise when the caregiver is unable to provide her services.

The caregiver should be allowed to assign her duties to another, perhaps an independent third party agency, if the need arises.

Because the family caregiver agreement is, in fact, an employment contract, it must be remembered that the usual rules regarding income taxes apply. The money that is earned by the caregiver is considered income. Furthermore, because the caregiver is considered an "employee" of the care recipient, the care recipient is required to pay all of the appropriate employer taxes for his employee. To assist with this, there are payroll agencies that can be called upon to prepare the payroll and provide the check to the caregiver as well as web-based services and software that can be purchased.

What becomes of the caregiver agreement if the care recipient moves into a facility such as assisted living or a nursing home? In this circumstance, it is important to remember that just because the care recipient may no longer live at home, it does not necessarily mean that the caregiver no longer has a job to do. Perhaps the hours that had been spent on personal care services will decrease, but the hours as a geriatric care manager or financial manager may conversely increase. Just because the care recipient is now living in a facility, the caregiver still has a role in his life. It is just as important that the caregiver remain on the scene and monitor the care that is now being provided by others. The caregiver is not duplicating the care that is being provided by the facility but rather overseeing the care, making certain there is no abuse, and enhancing the care recipient's life by doing so.

§ 5.3.3.
The Financial Plan

In many instances the family caregiver agreement is tied into an overall estate plan or long-term care plan for Medicaid planning purposes. Paying a family member for the care that she is providing is a permissible way to spend down the assets of the care recipient in preparation for applying for Medicaid. Even if Medicaid is not an issue, it is also a method for reducing the value of the care recipient's taxable estate so that there are less estate taxes to be paid upon death. However, in order for either scenario to work, it is important to make certain that the family caregiver agreement is properly drafted so that it can withstand a potential attack by either Medicaid or the Internal Revenue Service.

As noted previously, the first step in drafting an effective family caregiver agreement is to make certain that the payment to the caregiver is equal to the prevailing wages in the local community for the work being performed. This verifies that the caregiver is not being given extraordinary compensation above and beyond what is called for. Additionally, the caregiver should keep a contemporaneous time sheet or a log to show the number of hours she works on a weekly or monthly basis and the tasks she performs during those hours. Not only will this assist in dealings with government agencies but also in situations where other family members question the amount of time spent or the necessity of the services.

Another critical requirement is that the family caregiver agreement be in writing. Without a written agreement, any monies paid by the care recipient to the caregiver may be considered a "gift," which will disqualify the care recipient from Medicaid for some period of time. Furthermore, the Internal Revenue Service may also see the payments as "gifts" with potential gift and estate tax implications. The family caregiver agreement can call for one lump sum payment, or weekly or monthly payments determined by hours worked. An elder law or senior estate planning attorney in your state will best be able to advise which strategy you should use considering your state's Medicaid laws and your personal situation.

Finally, a written agreement offers protection to both the caregiver and the care recipient. Each will know what is required of the other so that there will be no question about whether the caregiver is providing the needed services.

§ 5.4.
DEALING WITH OTHER FAMILY MEMBERS

Discussions of money are often difficult amongst family members, and none more so than discussing the payment of a family member for the care of another. For this reason, it is very important for the family to meet and talk about what the care needs are and how those needs will be met.

A family discussion regarding how a parent's assets are going to be used to pay for his or her care is important in avoiding family friction down the road. The work that is needed to properly put together a family caregiver agreement can also help in this regard. When a physician puts down in writing the care needs of a parent, a family discussion can be had as to how those needs will be met. It is often that the out-of-town sibling does not understand how bad things have become for Mom or Dad and how much time and effort his sister or brother is expending in caring for Mom or Dad. The physician's report can help to establish just what a difficult job the caregiver is undertaking. Furthermore, when proposals are obtained from third-party caregivers for the costs involved in providing care, it is much easier for other family members to really appreciate the value of what the caregiver is providing.

One thing that may be considered in providing payment to the caregiver under a family caregiver agreement is that perhaps another family member should "hold the checkbook" and be the person who is responsible for payments to the caregiver. This is a way to keep others in the loop so that complaints cannot later be made of not understanding the costs involved. In short, by making sure that the family caregiver agreement is in writing with all terms clearly established and backed up by professionals lessens the chances of disagreements later. One goal for a family caregiver agreement is to preserve family relationships. If there is one thing that can lead to the destruction of those relationships, it is money.

§ 5.5.
WHEN A FAMILY CAREGIVER AGREEMENT IS NOT AN OPTION—OTHER AVAILABLE FINANCIAL ASSISTANCE

Quite clearly, not everyone is in a position where they can create a family caregiver agreement. For those who are struggling financially, there is some help available through the creation of the National Family Caregiver Support Program. The Older Americans Act, as amended in 2000, established and funded the National Family Caregiver Support Program (NFCSP), which was created to help relieve the financial hardships from the continual care by family caregivers (of any age) who act as unpaid caregivers for loved ones age 60 or older. The funding from the program is allocated to the states through a formula based on the proportionate share of the population aged 70 and above. As such, financial help for caregivers is primarily up to each individual state and/or community, with decisions based upon what can be afforded in the way of caregiver assistance at that particular time.

Most family caregivers who receive assistance from this program have been providing care for quite some time with little or no financial support. The types of support that this program offers include:

- Providing information to caregivers about available support services;
- Providing caregiver access to supportive services;
- Providing individual counseling, support groups, and caregiver training; and
- Providing respite care and supplemental services (such as emergency response systems and home modifications).

To find out specifics in your state, go to your state's Family Caregiver Support Program website and look under aging services. Contact your area's Agency on Aging if you have one that serves your area, or contact your county social services office and ask if they can help you find the right agency to contact.

§ 5.6. CONCLUSION

As the population continues to age and the costs of care continue to skyrocket, there will be more and more people stepping into the role of family caregiver. It is important to recognize the real work that these caregivers are providing not only to the family member in need of the care but to the entire family. It is also important to recognize the financial sacrifices that caregivers are called upon to give. One way to assist the caregiver is to visit an elder law or senior estate planning attorney who will be able to draft a well-written family caregiver agreement with an eye not only to providing the caregiver with fair payment for the services she is providing but also to assisting the care recipient with a means to pay for long-term care via Medicaid if and when that should be necessary.

For more information, visit the website of

Van Dyck Law, LLC

at **www.vandyckfirm.com**

[2] Lynn Feinberg et al., AARP Public Policy Institute, *Valuing the Invaluable: 2011 Update, The Growing Contributions and Costs of Family Caregiving,* assets.aarp.org/rgcenter/ppi/ltc/i51-caregiving.pdf

[3] *Id.*

[4] D'Vera Cohn & Paul Taylor, Pew Research Center, *Baby Boomers Approach 65 – Glumly,* http://www.pewsocialtrends.org/2010/12/20/baby-boomers-approach-65-glumly/

[5] National Alliance for Caregiving in collaboration with AARP, *Caregiving in the US, 2009* (Nov. 2009), p. 4, 11, www.caregiving.org/data/Caregiving_in_the_US_2009_full_report.pdf

[6] *Id.*

[7] Rice University News & Media, *Rice University Sociologists Calculate Caregivers' Risk of Living in Poverty* (Aug. 16, 2004), http://news.rice.edu/2004/08/16/rice-university-sociologists-calculate-caregivers-risk-of-living-in-poverty/

[8] US Department of Commerce, US Census Bureau, *Disability and American Families: 2000, Census 2000 Special Reports,* July 2005, p. 6, http://www.census.gov/population/www/cen2000/briefs/index.html#sr

[9] Lynn Feinberg et al., AARP Public Policy Institute, *Valuing the Invaluable: 2011 Update, The Growing Contributions and Costs of Family Caregiving,* assets.aarp.org/rgcenter/ppi/ltc/i51-caregiving.pdf

YOU DON'T HAVE TO WIN
THE LOTTERY TO PAY FOR
NURSING HOME CARE

CHAPTER 6

COMMON NURSING HOME CARE ISSUES

Margaret Madison Phelan, Esquire
and
*Karen L. Webber, Esquire, *CELA*

*Certified Elder Law Attorney by the National Elder Law Foundation

Margaret Madison Phelan and Karen L. Webber are elder law attorneys practicing law in the states of Oregon and Washington and are Accredited Attorneys by the Veterans Administration. Additionally, Margaret Madison Phelan is a member of the National Academy of Elder Law Attorneys.

Vera was admitted to a skilled nursing home after a week-long stay in a hospital for surgery to repair her broken hip. Upon admission, her family breathed a sigh of relief, thinking that after supervising her in-home care for the last few years, everything would be easier now that she was getting care in a skilled nursing home. However, shortly after admission, the nursing home called her daughter, wanting her daughter to sign some paperwork. Then some of Vera's personal property went missing. Once those issues were resolved, her family noticed that she was often restrained in the evenings. Her family then realized that oversight of Vera's care was still needed and started searching for answers to these and other issues. This article is meant to be a primer on the most common questions that come up from the time of admission to discharge.

§ 6.1. Introduction

§ 6.2. Admission & Payment

§ 6.3. Personal Property

§ 6.4. Quality of Care

§ 6.5. Discharge

§ 6.1.
INTRODUCTION

Family members of residents of skilled nursing facilities can advocate for the care provided to their loved ones. Meaningful advocacy comes from knowing what the law is and understanding the rights of nursing home residents. This chapter will pose the most common questions that arise when advocating for the care of a skilled nursing home resident. The questions range from admission, payment and personal property to quality of care and discharge issues.

This article is based upon federal laws, which govern the rights of all residents in skilled nursing facilities that accept payments from Medicare or Medicaid. Numerous other types of facilities now commonly also provide care such as adult family homes, assisted living facilities, and memory care (Alzheimer's) facilities. The laws regarding each of these types of facilities are not covered by federal law but are covered by the state law in which the facility is located. Many of the laws governing those facilities are similar to the laws covered herein.

§ 6.2.
ADMISSION & PAYMENT

Q. My father is to be admitted to a nursing home. The staff told me I had to sign the admission agreement as a "responsible party." What should I do?

A. Do not sign as a responsible party. Under federal law, a nursing home cannot require that a resident's family member or friend become personally liable for nursing home charges. The facility should be advised that you are not able to accept personal liability for your father's charges. If you are your father's attorney in fact under a durable power of attorney (DPOA), you should sign your name and follow it with either attorney in fact ("AIF") or "DPOA." If you are his conservator (or guardian of his estate), you should sign your name and follow it with "Conservator" (or "Guardian of the Estate") and provide the facility with a copy of your letters from the court authorizing you to act.

Q. Can a nursing home require that a resident pay the private pay rate for a certain period of time?

A. No. A Medicare or Medicaid-eligible nursing home resident cannot be required to stay a minimum number of days in the skilled nursing home, nor may the nursing home charge, solicit, or accept any gift, money, or donation in addition to the Medicare or Medicaid payment as a precondition to admission, expedited admission, or continued stay at the nursing home. Thus, the nursing home cannot require a resident who is eligible for Medicare or Medicaid to pay the private pay rate for a certain period of time as a condition of admission to the nursing home.

Q. Can a nursing home require that a resident post a deposit as a condition of admission?

A. The answer is different depending on whether the resident is paying his or her own costs or is Medicare or Medicaid eligible.

A Medicare or Medicaid eligible nursing home resident cannot be charged a deposit as a condition of admission to a nursing home. Neither may the nursing home charge, solicit, nor accept any gift, money, or donation in addition to the Medicare or Medicaid payment as a precondition to admission, expedited admission, or continued stay at the nursing home.

A nursing home can require a deposit from a private pay resident, but the nursing home must fully disclose in writing the amount of admission fees, deposits, prepaid charges, and minimum stay fees and the nursing home's policy concerning refunds of deposits, fees, and charges along with certain other requirements. Such disclosure must be in a language understood by the resident or the resident's representative.

Q. Does a nursing home resident lose his nursing home bed by going to a hospital for a period of time?

A. No. A nursing home resident may return to the first available bed in a semiprivate room in the nursing home after a relatively short hospital stay. The nursing home must advise the resident and his or her family of this right, in writing, at the time of admission and again at the time the resident is transferred to a hospital. This right applies to medical or mental health hospitalizations or therapeutic leaves.

A Medicaid-eligible resident has the right to return to the first available bed in a nursing home after a hospital stay of any length. If the resident requests that a specific bed be held, he or she may be charged a fee to hold that bed, but he or she may not be charged a bed-hold fee for the right to return to the first available bed in a semiprivate room.

Q. Can a nursing home provide a reduced level of care or services to a resident who receives financial assistance from the Medicaid program?

A. No. Nursing homes must establish and maintain identical policies and practices for all residents regardless of the resident's source of payment.

§ 6.3.
PERSONAL PROPERTY

Q. What can a nursing home resident do to help safeguard his or her personal property?

A. The nursing home is required to maintain a program to reduce loss and theft of residents' property. This program should be explained at the time the resident enters the nursing home.

A nursing home resident (or his or her personal representative) should make sure the nursing home inventories and marks his or her personal property when the resident first enters the nursing home, particularly eyeglasses and dentures. If the resident requests, new personal property brought into the nursing home should be added to the inventory and marked, and personal property removed from the nursing home should be removed from the inventory. The nursing home must provide a copy of this inventory to the resident upon request.

If the resident can afford the expense, he or she should provide a safe or a lock for a drawer or cabinet. The nursing home must provide a lockable container or lockable storage space for small items of personal property and if requested by a resident, a lock for the resident's drawer or cabinet. The resident must pay for the lock. The nursing home cannot require a resident to keep his or her valuables locked up, since the resident has the right to retain and use personal possessions.

A resident with dementia or Alzheimer's may well forget where he or she placed valuable items and should not have them with them. Often a low-cost substitute (i.e. costume ring for a ring with sentimental value) can be provided to the resident so they don't feel stripped of their possessions. Irreplaceable or valuable items should not be kept at the nursing home if the resident has another place to keep them.

Q. Is a nursing home financially responsible for a resident's lost or stolen personal property?

A. Yes. A nursing home cannot limit its potential liability for losses of a resident's personal property in an admission agreement or other document. The nursing home is required to account for any funds or property that it has agreed to hold and safeguard for a resident. It also must provide a secured area for personal property if requested to do so by the resident or resident's personal representative.

In most states, the nursing home must report allegations of misappropriation of residents' personal property to the state agency supervising the nursing home. Sometimes, homeowners' insurance will also provide a replacement for lost or stolen items.

§ 6.4.
QUALITY OF CARE

Q. The nursing home has recommended that my mother take medications which I think sedate her too much. Does she have to take them?

A. Your mother has the right to participate in and determine her plan of care to the extent possible. If she is unable to do this, her representative has the right to participate in and determine her care. The nursing home is also required to ensure that your mother or her representative has control over her care and treatment decisions. And your mother has the right to refuse treatment. Further, a nursing home cannot use medications for the purpose of discipline or convenience. Thus, your mother, or you as her representative if she is unable to make such decisions herself, can refuse medications.

Q. The nursing home wants to put side rails on my father's bed because he has fallen several times at night when he has used the bathroom after no one has responded to his call button. Does he have to accept the side rails?

A. A side rail is a physical constraint, and nursing homes cannot use physical constraints for purposes of discipline or convenience. Physical restraints may be used only as a last resort, or as a temporary measure, to ensure his physical safety and then only under a physician's order. It sounds like the nursing home may be choosing to use side rails instead of making sure staff responds to call buttons. In other words, they are using a physical restraint for the nursing home's convenience, and that is not permitted.

Q. My mother has Alzheimer's disease and becomes restless and sometimes agitated. Lately, she has been yelling quite a bit, which seems to bother the nursing home staff. They have told me that my mother must be moved by Saturday. Can the nursing home staff simply tell us to move my mother?

A. No. The nursing home must give your mother or her representative 30 days' written notice of the discharge. In a few situations, the period can be shortened. It can be less than 30 days only if

1. The health or safety of individuals in the nursing home would be endangered by your mother remaining in the nursing home;
2. Your mother's urgent medical needs require an immediate transfer or discharge; or
3. Your mother has not resided at the nursing home for 30 days.

Please note that a nursing home can only force a resident to move for one of the following reasons:

1. The resident has failed to make the required payment for her stay;

2. Transfer or discharge is necessary for your mother's welfare, and the nursing home cannot meet your mother's needs;

3. The safety or health of individuals in the nursing home, other than your mother, is endangered by your mother's actions; or

4. The nursing home ceases operations.

Q. What rehabilitation services and activities must a nursing home provide?

A. A nursing home must provide services and activities to attain or maintain the highest practicable physical and mental well-being of a resident. Residents on Medicare or Medicaid must be treated the same as private pay patients. A Medicare or Medicaid patient is entitled to medically-appropriate therapy services if these services are designed to improve a resident's condition or to maintain a resident's condition. In other words, the condition of a nursing home resident should not decline while he or she is in the nursing home unless the resident's condition is such that a decline is inevitable.

Rehabilitation services and activities may include, but are not limited to, physical therapy, occupational therapy, and speech therapy, including appropriate treatment for a resident with limited range of motion.

A nursing home must have both an activity program that follows a written, planned schedule and, for each resident, an individual activity plan consistent with the resident's other treatment. Activities should be designed to meet residents' preferences.

Q. What must a nursing home do to prevent or treat pressure sores?

A. A nursing home must prevent the decline of a resident's condition as much as possible, including the development of pressure sores and the treatment of pressure sores if they do occur. Preventive actions include, among other things, turning or shifting residents who are otherwise immobile in bed or in a wheelchair.

A resident with pressure sores must receive treatment to heal the sores and prevent infection. The nursing home must notify the resident's doctor when a pressure sore develops and when treatment of the pressure sore is ineffective and also must document the notification in the resident's record.

Q. How must a nursing home help a resident control his urine?

A. The nursing home must provide treatment that will help a resident attain or maintain the highest practicable physical, mental, and psychological well-being. The nursing home must ensure that a resident's abilities in the activities of daily living, including his or her ability to toilet, do not decline unless the resident's clinical condition indicates such decline was inevitable.

Q. How is a doctor involved in a nursing home resident's care?

A. Most facilities have a doctor who comes into the skilled nursing home five or more days a week. The doctor reviews a patient's chart with nursing staff and addresses concerns of the staff. Most often, the doctor does not make the rounds daily to visit each resident. Additionally, the nursing home must assure that a physician is available in case of an emergency. However, each resident has the right to select a personal physician. It is the resident's responsibility to travel to their personal physician if the physician is unwilling to come to the facility.

Q. How must a nursing home serve meals?

A. A nursing home must provide each resident with three meals a day. The nursing home must have table service available at a dining room outside the resident's room for those residents capable of eating at a table. The nursing home should also furnish adaptive utensils for those residents who need them. While a resident's preferences should be followed closely, the nursing home may make substitutions from appropriate food groups. The evening meal must not be separated from the following morning's breakfast by more than 14 hours. Additionally, the nursing home must provide a late breakfast or an alternative to breakfast for late risers.

Q. Are all nursing home residents required to follow the same schedule as every other resident?

A. No. A resident has the right to choose a schedule consistent with his or her interests. A nursing home must make "reasonable accommodations" to meet each resident's needs and preferences. The only exception is if the health or safety of the resident or other residents would be endangered. Thus, each resident may awaken and go to bed at the time he or she prefers.

The nursing home cannot use the excuse of not having enough staff members to accommodate a resident's requests to require the resident to conform to the nursing home's schedule. The nursing home is obligated to employ enough qualified employees to accommodate residents' needs.

Q. When can a nursing home resident receive visitors?

A. Generally, a nursing home resident may receive visitors at any reasonable time. A nursing home resident must be allowed "immediate access" to his or her immediate family or other relatives, meaning the immediate family members can visit at almost any time. Further, a nursing home cannot include a waiver of a resident's legal right to have visitors at any time in its admission agreement.

While a nursing home may recommend hours for visiting, those are only recommendations, not restrictions, on the hours during which family members or friends may visit residents. The only restrictions the nursing home may place on visiting hours are those that are reasonably necessary to protect the rights of other residents. However, the nursing home may require that visits be held at a place other than the resident's room, if needed, to protect a roommate's privacy or to not disturb a roommate.

The resident may impose his or her own restrictions on hours for visits and may choose not to allow certain people to visit or refuse to see someone.

Q. How can family members influence nursing home care?

A. Residents with friendly and appreciative family and friends who regularly visit on an irregular basis tend to receive the best care. Visiting the resident regularly at varying times allows the family member to observe the care provided by the nursing home at different times of the day. By varying the times of the visits, the nursing home staff will not be able to anticipate a family member's visit and provide more care or attention to the resident just prior to the expected visit.

Family members can organize a family council with families of the residents in the nursing home. Staff may attend family council meetings only by invitation from the family council. The nursing home must provide a meeting room for the family council. Family members can work with the council to pressure the nursing home into making changes that they have identified as necessary for their resident family member's care and that might be difficult to get changed working individually.

Q. How can a nursing home resident or friend negotiate to improve the quality or type of care being provided a resident without upsetting the facility?

A. If a resident or family member has a problem with the care or services provided by the nursing home, he or she should first discuss the problem with the nursing home staff. If the problem is not resolved, the resident or family member should be certain to attend the next care conference. If the issue is still not resolved, an inquiry should be made to see if the facility has a family council and attempt to resolve the dispute in that form. In addition, each state has a long-term-care ombudsman—with regional offices that can provide assistance in resolving disputes.

The ombudsman's representative works to assure that residents of nursing homes have their complaints or concerns about their treatment as a resident of a nursing home addressed and their rights protected. The ombudsman's office investigates complaints, responds to reports of abuse, works to promote dignity and autonomy and to improve the quality of life of nursing home residents. The service is free of charge and strictly confidential. In most states the phone number for the long-term care ombudsman can be obtained by a Google search or by calling the state's area Agency on Aging.

§ 6.5.
DISCHARGE

Q. The nursing home has given me a 30-day eviction notice, which says that my mother has to move because she is disturbing the other residents. Does she have to move?

A. No. A nursing home can only force a patient to move for one of the following reasons:

1. The resident has failed to make the required payment for her stay;

2. Transfer or discharge is necessary for your mother's welfare, and the nursing home cannot meet your mother's needs;

3. The safety or health of individuals in the nursing home, other than your mother, is endangered by your mother's actions; or

4. The nursing home ceases operations.

If any of the above conditions apply, the nursing home must give your mother or her representative 30 days' written notice of the discharge. The written notice may be given in less than 30 days as long as it is made as soon as practicable before discharge or transfer if:

1. The health or safety of individuals in the nursing home would be endangered by your mother remaining in the nursing home;

2. Your mother's urgent medical needs require an immediate transfer or discharge; or

3. Your mother has not resided at the nursing home for 30 days.

A patient's yelling, even if it bothers other residents or annoys the nursing home staff, is not enough by itself to allow the nursing home to force your mother to move. Even if your mother's behavior is severe enough to have her considered a difficult patient, that is not basis for the nursing home to force her to move. Her behavior would have to endanger the staff or other residents or herself. Even then, the nursing home must give your mother or her representative 30 days' notice unless the risk to others is so great that your mother must be moved sooner than 30 days. Additionally, the nursing home must provide sufficient preparation and orientation for your mother to ensure a safe and orderly transfer or discharge.

Q. Can the nursing home discharge my mother for not making progress in therapy or improving in condition?

A. No. Although nursing homes routinely discharge patients who are not making progress, improvement alone does not determine whether your mother should receive coverage to remain in the facility. Medicare providers must consider your condition as a whole to decide if you need ongoing treatment. Your mother *cannot* be denied coverage if continued professional care is necessary for her to:

1. Maintain her current level of functioning;

2. Prevent deterioration;

3. Preserve her current capabilities; or

4. Establish a safe and effective maintenance program.

Please note the importance of participation in the treatment plan prescribed by her doctor. In some cases, individuals are denied coverage because their condition is not expected to improve when, in fact, the individuals are not going to therapy. Failure to participate makes discharge more likely unless conditions, such as depression, present a barrier to participation.

Q. My spouse passed away on the 22ⁿᵈ of the month. Can the skilled nursing home require that I pay for a full month's care?

A. Federal nursing home law provides that residents cannot be charged a deposit or be required to stay a minimum number of days in a skilled nursing home. Assuming a resident's personal property is promptly removed, the skilled nursing facility cannot charge for additional days thereafter.

For more information, visit the website of

Phelan Webber & Associates

at **www.madphelan.com**

DON'T LET THE UNKNOWNS ABOUT
SOCIAL SECURITY DRIVE YOU CRAZY

CHAPTER 7

SOCIAL SECURITY PLANNING

Paul J. Stano, Esquire

Like many middle-aged couples, Tom and Denise were excited about the prospect of retirement. They envisioned leisurely days at the beach, long-distance traveling, and spending time with their grandchildren. So when Tom, at age 62, was offered early retirement by his employer, he and Denise jumped at the opportunity.

They did rough calculations and decided that their Social Security benefits, along with their investment portfolio, would provide a comfortable-enough retirement nest egg. Unfortunately, by Tom claiming Social Security benefits at 62, which is the earliest age eligible, the couple had dimmed some of the luster from their golden years.

By opting to take benefits at 62 instead of waiting until his full retirement age, which ranges between 65 and 67 years, depending on when a person was born, Tom permanently reduced his monthly Social Security check by 25 percent. And because spousal benefits are generally

50 percent of the primary (or higher earner's) amount, the couple had also shortchanged Denise's lifetime benefits by tens of thousands of dollars.

Social Security is an integral part of virtually every American's retirement program. Before electing a Social Security option that could have significant financial consequences, married couples and individuals should diligently assess their choices.

§ 7.1.
INTRODUCTION

For many people, retirement planning consists mainly of taking the occasional look at their 401(k) and IRA statements. But if you are among the 96 percent of workers who are covered under Social Security, it's in your best interests to understand how the system works and what you and your family will receive from Social Security when you retire.

Social Security is one of the few sources of income that's guaranteed to last for life and keep pace with inflation. Although Social Security provides 50 percent of the income for more than half of married retired couples and about 20 percent for high-income couples, many people are unsure of how Social Security fits into their overall retirement plans. A key reason for the uncertainty is that Social Security's monthly benefits depend on numerous variables, including when you retire, how much you and your spouse earned, and whether you work during your retirement. This chapter will discuss some of the challenges of Social Security planning and offer strategies for collecting the maximum benefits you're entitled to receive.

§ 7.2.
THE ROOTS OF SOCIAL SECURITY

Nearly eight decades old, the Social Security system has evolved to meet the changing dynamics of American demographics, work patterns, and lifestyles.

In the midst of the Great Depression in 1935, President Franklin D. Roosevelt established the Social Security Act (SSA) as part of his New Deal. As the nation struggled through its worst economic crisis, millions of Americans lost their jobs and depleted their savings. Roosevelt, saying he was concerned about the plight of "young people who have come to wonder what would be their lot when they came to old age," created a system that would provide a source of income for the unemployed, the disabled, and retirees.

The original intent of the SSA was to provide benefits to retirees and some unemployed people, but Social Security is now typically viewed as a safety net for retired and disabled Americans. SSA also provides death benefits to taxpayers' dependents.

Initially, the Social Security benefit for retirees was not designed to be permanent. The SSA was supposed to be a temporary "relief" program that would eventually be supplanted as people were able to obtain retirement income. There were also limits on the unemployed who received benefits. Certain job categories were not covered by the SSA, including agricultural and domestic workers, government employees, and many nurses, hospital employees, librarians, teachers, and social workers.

In 1939, the SSA was amended to include survivors' benefits and benefits for the retiree's spouse and children. Social Security was expanded in 1950 to cover all nongovernment workers, including the self-employed. Three decades later, civilian federal workers were eligible for Social Security benefits.

The addition of disability insurance occurred in 1956. This change provided monthly cash benefits for disabled workers and their dependents who had paid into the system and met certain work requirements.

In 1965, President Lyndon Johnson signed legislation that amended the Social Security Act to include Medicare and Medicaid. Medicare is a basic program of hospital insurance for persons aged 65 and older, as well as a supplementary medical insurance program to aid the elderly in paying doctor bills and other health-care bills. Medicaid is a state and federal program that mainly serves the health-care needs of low-income individuals and families.

As a mandatory retirement program, Social Security operates on a "pay-as-you-go" system in which payroll taxes from current workers are used to fund benefits for retirees and those who have disabilities.

At this writing, **there are currently 2.8 workers for each Social Security beneficiary. By 2033, the U.S. Social Security Administration estimates there will be 2.1 workers for each beneficiary.**

Social Security payroll taxes are deposited into trust funds managed by the U.S. Treasury. Social Security and disability benefits are paid from these funds, which are invested in Treasury bonds. There have been 11 years in which the Social Security program did not take in enough payroll (FICA) taxes to pay the current year's benefits. To meet the deficit, the Treasury sold trust fund bonds. As the huge baby boomer generation—those people born between 1946 and 1964—transitions from the workforce into retirement, some analysts say the Social Security system will be pushed further into a deficit situation.

While the Social Security system may be perceived to be on uncertain fiscal footing, it remains a crucial element of many people's retirement funding. Government statistics show that[10]:

- **In 2013, almost 58 million Americans will receive $816 billion in Social Security benefits.**
- Nine out of ten individuals age 65 and older receive Social Security benefits.
- Social Security benefits represent about 39 percent of the income of the elderly.
- Among elderly Social Security beneficiaries, 53 percent of married couples and 74 percent of unmarried persons receive 50 percent or more of their income from Social Security.
- Among elderly Social Security beneficiaries, 23 percent of married couples and about 46 percent of unmarried

persons rely on Social Security for 90 percent or more of their income.

§ 7.3.
SOCIAL SECURITY: THE BEDROCK RETIREMENT PLAN

In recent decades, employers have trended away from defined-benefit pension plans, which guarantee a certain benefit upon retirement, in favor of defined-contribution plans such as 401(k) programs, which pay a benefit based on a worker's contributions and the rate of return they earn.

Social Security, for most workers, is the only source of guaranteed retirement income that is not subject to investment risk or financial market fluctuations.

And because Social Security isn't means-tested (it doesn't reduce or deny benefits to people if their income or assets exceed a certain level), the program is the foundation of retirement protection for workers of nearly all earning levels.

In 2012, an estimated 57 million people, or about one in every six US residents, collected Social Security benefits[11]. Three-quarters of them received benefits as retirees or elderly widow(er)s, while another 19 percent received disability insurance benefits, and 4 percent received benefits as young survivors of deceased workers[12].

§ 7.3.1.
Who Is Eligible for Social Security?

In general, a worker must be at least age 62 and have accrued 40 quarters or 10 years of "covered employment" to be eligible for retirement benefits. Retirees become eligible for benefits on the first full month after their 62nd birthday. For example, if you turn 62 on May 5, you become eligible for benefits on June 1.

Covered employment means you have a job in which you and your employer pay Social Security taxes. If you are self-employed, you are responsible for paying both the employer and employee shares. There still exist several large employee groups, including federal government employees and railroad workers, who are not covered by Social Security. Since they had already established pension plans before Social Security was enacted, Congress decided to exclude them from the new retirement program. Also, at the time of Social Security's inception, legislators believed they could not mandate a federal pension plan such as Social Security on state and local government entities, so employees of those agencies were allowed to choose whether they wanted to participate in Social Security. Many state and local entities established their own pension plans, which operated independently of Social Security.

Nowadays, the only large groups of US workers not covered by Social Security are railroad workers (who are covered by the Railroad Retirement Board)[13], a small number of older federal government employees[14], and about 27.5 percent of state and local public employees[15].

As a note, Social Security "quarters" are also referred to as "credits." You earn credits when you work and pay Social Security taxes. The credits are based on the amount of your earnings. In 2012, workers received one credit for each $1,130 of earnings, up to the maximum of four credits per year. Each year the amount of earnings needed for credits goes up slightly as average earnings levels increase. Generally, a person needs 40 credits to be eligible for benefits.

Q: What happens if you don't accumulate 40 credits by the time you wish to retire?

A: Put simply, if you don't have 40 credits, you cannot receive Social Security retirement benefits based on your own work record. If this is the case, your family will also not be eligible to receive benefits based on your record. To be eligible for retirement benefits, you must continue working in Social Security-covered employment, either full-time or part-time, until you have earned 40 credits.

§ 7.3.2.
Maximizing Family Benefits

When you qualify for Social Security retirement benefits, certain members of your family may be eligible for benefits. To get family benefits, a spouse, divorced spouse, or child of an insured family member does not have to earn any credits on their own. Their eligibility is based on the insured family member having at least 40 credits. While there are limits on the total retirement benefits a family can get, eligible dependents may include:

- A spouse who is 62 years of age or older
- A spouse who is under 62 years if he/she is caring for a child who is under 16 years or disabled
- Unmarried children under 18 years

- Unmarried children age 18–19, if they are full time students in high school
- Children age 18 and older who are severely disabled from a condition that started before age 22
- A divorced spouse who is unmarried, age 62 or older, and married to you for at least ten years. You must have been divorced for at least two years.
- Grandchildren may be eligible if they depend on you financially. For example, if the grandchild's parents don't provide support due to death or disability, the grandchild may qualify for Social Security benefits on your work record.

§ 7.3.3.
How Do I Calculate My Benefits?

The average Social Security retirement benefit is $1,230 per month (in 2012)[16], but the exact amount you'll get every month depends on how much you've earned over your lifetime and how old you are when you start collecting Social Security.

The Social Security benefit calculation is somewhat complex. But, in general, out of a worker's entire earnings from age 22 to 62, the highest 35 years of indexed earnings are used to compute a monthly benefit. Actual earnings are adjusted or "indexed" to make sure benefits reflect the rise in the standard of living that occurs during a worker's lifetime.

For help in calculating your projected monthly benefit, you can use Social Security's online tools at www.ssa.gov/planners/benefitcalculators.htm. The tools include the Quick Calculator, which provides an instant but rough estimate. To use the Quick Calculator, simply input your date of birth and this year's earnings.

For a more precise calculation, use Social Security's Retirement Estimator, which incorporates your actual earnings record on file with the Social Security Administration.

The American Association of Retired Persons (AARP) also offers an online Social Security benefit calculator at www.aarp.org/work/ social-security/social-security-benefits-calculator. AARP's calculator can help estimate your Social Security benefits and also provide guidance on the best age to claim Social Security.

§ 7.4.
When Filing for Social Security, It Pays to Delay

Statistically, nearly half of all Americans claim their Social Security benefits at age 62[17], which is the earliest that one can collect. For some, filing early is a financial necessity. But for others, the decision to collect their benefits as soon as possible is often based on somewhat nebulous reasoning, including the perception that the Social Security system will be changed, cut, or even become insolvent, or that money can be better invested in a mutual fund or other private account. Somewhat surprisingly, many financial planners have done little to encourage their clients to consider delaying their Social Security filing.

The fact is that people who begin collecting Social Security at age 62 are locking in the lowest monthly benefit. Be aware that individuals who begin receiving benefits before their full retirement age (FRA) of 66 may experience a benefit reduction of as much as 30 percent[18]. In the case of early retirement, the benefit is reduced 5/9 of 1 percent for each month before normal retirement age, up to 36 months[19]. If the number of months exceeds 36, then the benefit is further reduced 5/12 of 1 percent per month[20]. The reason for the reduction is that early retirees actuarially end up getting benefits for an additional 48 months.

If you can delay filing until you reach your FRA—or even until you turn 70 (when you'll get the maximum amount of benefits)— you can significantly boost your lifetime payout. Each year that you delay claiming your benefits past your full retirement age, up to 70, your benefit ticks about 8 percent higher[21]. This step-up is due to what the Social Security Administration calls "delayed retirement credits."

Of course, working past 62 isn't always practical, especially for people with physically demanding jobs or for those who have health issues. However, those who are able to wait until age 70 to collect Social Security will receive benefits that are 76 percent higher than if they had started collecting at age 62[22].

Additionally, in the case of a married couple, where one spouse earned less over his or her work life, that higher benefit shifts over to the surviving spouse, in full for life, if the primary beneficiary dies.

This chart[23] illustrates the advantages of delaying your Social Security payout.

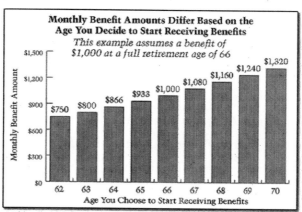

133

§ 7.4.1.
Filing Strategies for Married Couples

When it comes to Social Security planning, married couples may have options that singles don't. There are specific strategies that can help couples maximize their Social Security benefits. However, couples also need to avoid common pitfalls, including the mistaken belief that spouses cannot both collect full benefits; (they can).

One oft-repeated error is this scenario: The husband, who is the higher earner, believes he has greater odds of dying before his wife. So, because he doesn't want to lose out on any of his Social Security entitlement, he claims his benefits as early as possible and his wife delays.

But this scenario, in most cases, is the exact opposite of what should occur. If the husband files for Social Security as soon as he's eligible and then dies before his wife, he's locked in a reduced benefit for her. A better approach would be for the husband to delay his claim. That leaves the wife with the option of claiming the husband's higher benefit when he dies (or at his later filing age). In a case where the wife dies first, the husband simply keeps his own benefit.

§ 7.4.2.
"File and Suspend" Can Yield Rewards

A technique that can potentially yield the maximum benefit for married couples is the "file and suspend" strategy. In this scenario, let's say the husband is the breadwinner. When he reaches his FRA of 66 (or 67, if born in 1960 or later), he can file for benefits but suspend collecting them. This allows his lower-earning spouse (who must be 62 or older) to claim a spousal benefit, while the breadwinner's unclaimed benefit continues to grow.

If the husband continues to work and starts collecting benefits at 70, he still gets the maximum benefit amount, just as if he had filed at that age. However, because he filed at age 66, his wife became eligible immediately to start collecting one-half of the husband's benefit amount. Keep in mind that the wife will receive a reduced payout if she starts collecting before she reaches her FRA.

§ 7.4.3.
The "Restricting Claims" Technique

Two-career couples with similar income levels may want to consider a strategy in which one spouse "restricts" his or her Social Security claim to spousal benefits only. This works only when the other spouse is collecting benefits.

It works like this: The husband, in this example, turns age 66. He files for Social Security benefits but requests that the claim be restricted to spousal benefits. His benefit amount will be half of his wife's Social Security payout. Now the husband can continue to work without worrying about losing any Social Security benefits to the earnings cap.

When the husband reaches age 70, he can file for his own retirement benefit, which should be larger. The end result is that the husband has received spousal benefits for four years (age 66 to 70) at essentially no cost to him. And by delaying his own retirement benefits for four more years, his monthly payout will have grown significantly.

The strategy of restricting a claim to spousal benefits can also be used by divorced couples. To be eligible to collect on your ex-wife or ex-husband, you must have been married for at least ten years and divorced for at least two years, and you may not be currently married. You can collect benefits as early as age 62 (earnings-cap limits apply if you continue to work), as long as your former spouse is old enough to be eligible for benefits, even if he or she has not yet collected them.

But if you can wait until age 66, you have the option of restricting your Social Security payout to spousal benefits only, which then allows your own benefits to accrue on a delayed basis. You can then switch to your own benefit (assuming it's larger) at age 70.

Different rules apply for widows. They may collect survivor benefits as early as age 60 (rather than age 62), but they are still subject to the annual earnings-test limits if they continue working while receiving benefits. However, if they are entitled to retirement benefits based on their own work history, they may collect survivor benefits first and switch to retirement benefits later, or vice versa, depending on which will provide a higher benefit.

§ 7.5.
WHAT HAPPENS IF I WORK DURING RETIREMENT?

Collecting Social Security benefits should not inhibit you from working. When you reach your full retirement age, you can work and earn as much as you want and still receive your full Social Security benefit payment. If you are younger than full retirement age and if your earnings exceed certain dollar amounts, your Social Security checks will be reduced by $1 for every $2 you earn over an annual limit ($15,720 in 2015)[24].

But contrary to what you may have heard, you don't actually lose that money. At full retirement age, Social Security will begin compensating you with a larger payment for the benefits that were withheld, and you'll receive that higher payment for the rest of your life. If you are long-lived, there's a good chance you'll increase the total value of your lifetime benefits.

§ 7.6.
INTEGRATING MEDICARE WITH SOCIAL SECURITY PLANNING

Effective Social Security planning includes the coordination of Medicare coverage. Keep in mind that Social Security eligibility begins at age 62, but Medicare enrollment does not begin until age 65. If you are considering an early retirement, make sure you have alternate insurance in place, either privately or through a spouse.

It's not uncommon for an early retiree to confuse the starting ages of Social Security with Medicare. Additionally, people who have been covered by corporate health insurance are sometimes not aware of the high costs and the limitations of private-pay insurance. If you forego health insurance, you may be putting yourself and your family at risk for enormous financial consequences.

For people 65 and older, Medicare serves as our nation's health insurance program. Medicare consists of four parts: Part A (hospital coverage); Part B (medical insurance); Part C (Medicare Advantage) and Part D (prescription drugs).

Certain people younger than age 65 can also qualify for Medicare, including those who have disabilities, permanent kidney failure, or amyotrophic lateral sclerosis (ALS).

Medicare is financed by a portion of the payroll taxes paid by workers and their employers. It also is financed in part by monthly premiums deducted from Social Security checks.

New Medicare enrollees have a seven-month window to sign up, starting three months before their 65th birthday. If you delay beyond this time period, you may incur penalties. You can enroll directly by contacting the Social Security Administration. You also have the option of enrolling through a private insurer that offers a Medicare Advantage plan, which is basic Medicare plus a few extra features like dental and vision benefits.

Upon joining Medicare, each beneficiary pays a monthly premium along with deductibles and copayments. Medicare pays the rest of the covered health-care services. Although the program is designed to help defray the cost of health care, it does not cover some medical services or the cost of most long-term care.

To fill in Medicare's coverage gaps, participants can purchase supplemental policies called Medigap plans, which are sold by private companies. To assist consumers in choosing among various Medigap plans, the policies have been standardized and are identified in most states by letters ranging from A to N. Every Medigap policy must follow federal and state laws designed to protect purchasers, and they must be clearly identified as "Medicare Supplement Insurance." The policies offer a wide range of benefits to suit various needs and budgets.

Another significant gap in Medicare coverage are the provisions for long-term care. Medicare generally only pays for brief stays at long-term care facilities that are for rehabilitation or recovery. Medicare pays less than 15 percent of nursing home expenses nation-wide and even less for costs associated with assisted living and home health care. Retirees who are concerned about the increasing costs of long-term care may want to explore various insurance products that can help minimize the financial burden of a lengthy nursing home stay.

Medicare enrollees who don't specify otherwise will most likely be enrolled in Original Medicare, the traditional fee-for-service program offered directly through the federal government. With Original Medicare, you are covered to go to just about any doctor or hospital in the country.

People can also choose to get their Medicare benefits instead through a Medicare private health plan (such as an HMO or PPO). These plans, which are also called "Medicare Advantage" plans, must offer at least the same benefits as Original Medicare but can have different rules, costs, and coverage restrictions. They can also offer additional benefits. You may not enroll in a Medigap plan if you are enrolled in a Medicare Advantage plan.

§ 7.7.
CONCLUSION

Social Security is controversial and often misunderstood. When planning for retirement, it's important to take the time to understand Social Security's vital role in your and your family's financial future. Deciding when and how to file for Social Security benefits depends on a number of personal factors, including your current cash needs, your health and expected longevity, your projected financial needs, whether you plan to work in retirement, and your various income sources.

Social Security is ever changing and increasingly complex. As you assess your various options, you'll find a great deal of information on the Social Security Administration website (www.ssa.gov). Not all people will need to consult a financial advisor to assist in their Social Security decision-making process. You may feel more comfortable consulting an attorney or other professional, particularly if you have questions in other areas of retirement and estate planning.

For more information, visit the website of

Stano Law

at **www.stanolaw.com**

[10] These statistics are taken verbatim from US Social Security Administration, *Social Security Basic Facts*, http://www.ssa.gov/pressoffice/basicfact.htm

[11] US Social Security Administration, *Social Security Basic Facts*, http://www.ssa.gov/pressoffice/basicfact.htm

[12] *Id.*

[13] US Railroad Retirement Board, *An Agency Overview* (Jan. 2013), http://www.rrb.gov/opa/agency_overview.asp

[14] US Social Security Administration, *Retirement Planner: Federal Government Employment*, http://www.ssa.gov/retire2/fedgovees.htm

[15] US Congressional Research Service, *Social Security: Mandatory Coverage of New State and Local Government Employees*, p. 1 (R41936; July 25, 2011), by Dawn Nuschler et al., http://www.nasra.org/resources/CRS%202011%20Report.pdf

[16] US Social Security Administration, *Average Monthly Social Security Benefit for a Retired Worker*, http://ssa-custhelp.ssa.gov/app/answers/detail/a_id/13/~/average-monthly-social-security-benefit-for-a-retired-worker

[17] US Congressional Research Service, *Fact Sheet: The Social Security Retirement Age*, p. 4 (R41962; Jan. 24, 2013), by Gary Sidor, https://www.fas.org/sgp/crs/misc/R41962.pdf

[18] US Social Security Administration, *Social Security Benefits: Early or Late Retirement?*, http://www.ssa.gov/oact/quickcalc/early_late.html

[19] *Id.*

[20] *Id.*

[21] US Congressional Research Service, *Fact Sheet: The Social Security Retirement Age*, p. 4 (R41962; Jan. 24, 2013), by Gary Sidor, https://www.fas.org/sgp/crs/misc/R41962.pdf

[22] AARP Bulletin, Jane Bryant Quinn, *Social Security, Longevity Insurance: Are you better off with early-but-lower payments or later-but-higher payments?* (Feb. 3, 2011), http://www.aarp.org/work/social-security/info-02-2011/financially_speaking_social_security_your_longevity_insurance.html

[23] US Social Security Administration, *When To Start Receiving Retirement Benefits*, SSA Publication No. 05-10147, ICN 480136 (Aug. 2012), http://www.socialsecurity.gov/pubs/10147.pdf

[24] US Social Security Administration, *Retirement Planner: Getting Benefits While Working*, http://www.socialsecurity.gov/retire2/whileworking.ht

"DO YOU HAVE ANY BUSINESS SUCCESSION PLANS?"

CHAPTER 8

WHERE'S MY U-HAUL?
BUSINESS SUCCESSION PLANNING

Julieanne E. Steinbacher, Esquire
and
Samantha K. Wolfe, Esquire, LL.M. in Taxation

Julieanne E. Steinbacher is certified as an Elder Law Attorney by the National Elder Law Foundation, and both Julieanne E. Steinbacher and Samantha K. Wolfe are Accredited Attorneys by the Veterans Administration.

§ 8.1.
INTRODUCTION

Like most people, I hate moving. If you ever have to move, my sister, Krista, is the greatest vehicle packer I know. She has this ability to see an object and know exactly how to situate it in the vehicle to maximize space and minimize damage. She doesn't have to pack and repack either. You give her time to look at everything that has to fit into the vehicle, and she can get everything in the car on the first try. I call it spacimization. Spacimization is an amazing talent. Sadly, I don't have this talent, but I have witnessed it countless times.

For most people, spacimization isn't technically a word, but it is at the Wolfe house. Our family has moved a lot of people, and it has become apparent that some members of the Wolfe family have the talent and others don't. We had to invent a title for this talent because so few people have it. Those who don't have the talent end up being the gopher during every move. The gophers are the ones that actually do all the work, while those with the spacimization talent get to stand by the vehicle and boss everyone else around. I'm petty, I know. As you may have guessed, I don't have the talent.

Krista and I lived together in college, and one year after a particularly tough finals week, we decided that we were so over the semester and wanted to leave State College in the dust. The problem was that nothing in our apartment had been packed. Krista, never one to let something like packing up our apartment stand in her way, immediately got to it. I helped, almost willingly. Because I don't have spacimization, I got the chore of carrying all the apartment furnishings out to the living room so that Krista could see what items she had to pack. Basically, she stood around and looked at the items while I moved everything into the living room. Then, once she had a plan of where everything would go in the car, she went down to the car to pack as I brought items to her.

The one item that I was most worried about in the move was our television. It wasn't a big screen television, and it really wasn't that expensive, but it had been given to us, and, like many college girls, I regularly watched daytime soaps to get through the rigors of finals week. That television was my only way to figure out what was happening on General Hospital every day. Krista recognized that daytime television was the key to keeping my sanity during finals week. So she made sure that anything that was packed in the Volkswagen Jetta revolved around that television. We were both determined that the television would not be busted during the move.

Twenty treks up the stairs and buckets of sweat later (the sweat was all mine), our television was nestled under four blankets and between five pillows, and State College, Pennsylvania, was disappearing in our rearview mirror. The television safely made the trip and the next year during finals time both Krista and I were happy that she had used her spacimization to pack the car.

I have come to the conclusion that spacimization is somewhat genetic. My dad is the king of spacimization. He taught Krista well. Any time we went on vacation, my dad would ask my mom which items my mom was most concerned about and then would pack the vehicle around those items. All of those items made it through the trip unscathed.

I am reminded of Krista and Dad's spacimization ability any time I am meeting with clients to discuss business succession planning. Basically, business succession planning is packing for a road trip or move. It is identifying the business as the cherished asset and then ensuring that it makes the move intact. If business succession planning is like packing for *a move, and we know there are going to be bumps and rough terrain, why don't we prepare for the transition better?*

I am not asking these questions rhetorically. I have seen firsthand what happens when there is not a proper business succession plan in place. My dad and I like to joke about how I got a crash course in business succession planning before I turned fourteen, although technically it was more like a how not to do a business succession plan.

My dad grew up on a dairy farm in Maryland. He lived with his aunt and uncle and helped out on their farm. He still complains about the 2 a.m. milkings and loves to say that my sisters and I don't know what work is because we never had to milk the cows before going to school. He regales all of these stories with that mischievous glint in his eye, and I know he loved it. Since before I can remember, my uncle was sick with Parkinson's disease. When he died in the early 90s, my Aunt Katherine decided it was time to talk about what would happen to the farm when she passed away. She knew how much my dad had loved living at the farm and wanted to make sure that the legacy would go to my dad upon her death. It was important to her to move it to my dad in the best way. She wanted it nestled in four blankets and surrounded by five pillows.

I remember sitting at our dinner table listening to my dad and Aunt Katherine hash out all the details. They were on the right track to implementing a proper business plan. They had great intentions to pull off a seamless transition, but through a series of bad circumstances and some bad advice from my Aunt Katherine's attorney, the business succession plan never got off the ground. My dad really doesn't like to talk about it. This man is the king of spacimization and can inventory everything that will be taken on vacation. He isolates the important items and situates everything in the vehicle to make the move successful, but somehow he was on the receiving end of a poorly executed business plan. It would be like Krista packing our Volkswagen Jetta and busting my television during the move before it gets to the destination. I would open the trunk of the car and just see pieces of the television screen shattered on the floor of the trunk.

If you take a step back, you can learn a lot from my dad's circumstances. Knowing what I know now and having the experiences I have had advising clients, if my dad had asked me to create his business succession plan, I would have asked six basic questions. I'm sure these six questions would have sparked additional questions, but it would have started the wheels turning and would have laid the foundation for a business succession plan.

—Samantha K. Wolfe,
Esquire, LL.M. in Taxation

§ 8.2
THE SIX SUCCESSION QUESTIONS

Question #1: Why is a business succession plan needed?

When Krista packs a vehicle, she always takes inventory of what she has to pack and then makes a plan about the best way to transition the items for the move. The plan may not be written, but you better believe that she has a plan about the order and position of each item in the vehicle. Similarly, a business succession plan is needed to identify the goals of the transition and to facilitate a smooth transition of the business and all of the business's assets.

When my dad and Aunt Katherine met with the attorney, the attorney didn't ask what was most important to both my dad and Aunt Katherine. There was no plan. If the attorney had asked my dad what he and Aunt Katherine wanted to accomplish, my dad would have said to transfer the farm to him while paying the minimal amount of tax. The attorney could have mapped out the steps that would have needed to be taken in order to accomplish that goal.

A major component of a successful business succession plan is identifying the future decision-makers. In my dad's case, he has a brother that lives out of state and a sister, neither of whom spent a lot of time working on the farm. Aunt Katherine wanted to ensure that my dad had the ability to make the decisions regarding the farm since he had invested so much in its success. In order to maintain healthy relationships between siblings, it would have been helpful for the attorney working with Aunt Katherine to include not only my dad but also his brother and sister in the discussion about the transition of the farm to the next generation.

Because of the complexities of a business succession plan, the emotional facet of business succession planning is often overlooked. It is important to remember that you need to consider not only the mechanics of the transition but also the emotional ramifications of the transition. The first thing Krista does before starting to pack is make the gopher (me) bring all the items that will be making the move to one place so she can inventory it all. Then, the first question that Krista always asks is "What is the most important item I will be packing?" She asks because she understands that there is usually a particular item that is valued more than the other items. When Krista and I were moving, the television was most important to me. So, that is what Krista centered the entire move around. Likewise, when you are creating a business succession plan, consider not only how to get the business from one owner to another, but what is most important to each owner.

Question #2: What mechanism do I use to facilitate the business succession plan?

When most people think business succession plan, they think buy-sell agreement, but a buy-sell agreement is only one of the ways to transition a business.

A few options to transition a business include outright gifting, including a specific bequest in the last will and testament, using patterned gifting to gradually transition the business to the next generation, gifting to different types of trusts, or using a buy-sell agreement.

The simplest business succession plan is to either gift the business outright when you want to transition the business to someone else, or to include a provision in the last will and testament specifying who will receive the business upon the death of the current owner. Experience has taught, however, that the simplest plan is not always the best business succession plan. Remember, it boils down to whether the business succession plan accomplishes the goals of the current owner and the future owner.

In my dad's circumstances, the attorney heard my dad when he said he wanted to keep the business succession plan simple, but he missed it when my dad and Aunt Katherine stressed that the most important goal was to transition the farm to my dad while minimizing tax for both my dad and Aunt Katherine. Additionally, it would have been helpful for the attorney to explain that there is more than one type of tax and if you choose an option to reduce one type of tax, you may be increasing tax liability for a different type of tax.

In general, most people want a simple business succession plan, but more importantly, they want a successful business succession plan. My guess is that most clients would forfeit the simplest plan in favor of the complex plan if it meets all of their goals. On the flip side, I try never to make a plan more complex than it needs to be.

Question #3: How does the business transition occur?

This question sounds much more difficult than it actually is. The question should really be "Is the business being gifted to the next generation or will there be a sale?" For my dad, Aunt Katherine determined that Dad had already paid her for the farm through the years of work he did on the farm. She generously wanted to give my dad a part of the legacy he had helped create. In Aunt Katherine's situation, she had other assets that she was going to give to my dad's siblings. Sometimes there may not be other assets for the beneficiaries; there may only be the business for the future generations.

In my experience, a sale seems to be more prevalent in situations when the only asset that the client has is the business. In those circumstances, the client will gift part of the asset to a child and then the child will have to buy out the siblings' shares of the business.

Just remember to consider the ramifications to every member of the family. How does the sale or gift affect each individual?

Question #4: How is the business transition funded?

If a business will be gifted to the next generation, this question is obviously not needed; but if there is a buy-sell agreement or a sale that will occur, this question is vital.

Typically, with a buy-sell agreement, the transition is funded with life insurance. The buy-sell agreement may be an entity purchase agreement, a cross purchase agreement, or a hybrid agreement. If the buy-sell agreement is an entity purchase agreement, the business purchases life insurance policies on the business owners, and when a business owner dies, the business buys back the ownership interest from the business owner's estate or family members. If the buy-sell agreement is a cross purchase agreement, the business owners purchase life insurance policies on the life of the other business owner. If the buy-sell agreement is a hybrid agreement, the business usually has the first option to buy the deceased business owner's ownership interest. If the business opts not to exercise that option, the remaining business owners have the option to purchase the deceased business owner's interest in the business.

Even if there is not a buy-sell agreement in place, if the business is transitioning to the next generation through a sale, then consider the source to fund the sale. Also, consider whether the sale will occur in a single transaction or through a structured sale. Does there need to be some sort of payment plan?

For my dad, Aunt Katherine did have other assets that went through her estate that would have provided some funds to facilitate a purchase of the farm. I have met with multiple clients where that is not the case, so one of the purposes for the business succession plan is to identify how to accomplish the transition.

When you think about how a business succession plan is funded, consider how my sister packs the vehicle. The funds of a business succession plan are similar to the blankets and pillows Krista uses to pad each item in the vehicle. The padding around the television is not the item that needs to be moved, but offers the support and cushion to help the television move from one place to another without damage. You wouldn't consider moving treasured assets without the proper cushion and padding, and you shouldn't transition a business without considering what is going to fund the transition.

Question #5: What triggers the transition of the business?

Think the three D's—death, divorce, and disability. There can be other triggering events, but those are the big ones to consider.

A proper business succession plan needs to address what triggers the transition or the start of the transition. The majority of the clients I meet with consider transition upon death, but not many consider what will happen to the business if a business owner becomes disabled or gets divorced.

During the last year of Aunt Katherine's life, her health was not good at all. She wasn't able to do much regarding the farm, but she had the experience and knowledge to advise my dad when he was making decisions; so although the attorney did not draft the business succession plan to address what would happen if Aunt Katherine would become disabled, in my dad's situation, he probably wouldn't have wanted her disability to trigger the transition of the farm. If, however, the circumstances were different, and Aunt Katherine didn't have the knowledge to advise my dad, it may have been more beneficial for Aunt Katherine's disability to trigger the transition of the farm. For example, if my dad had needed more assistance with manual labor of the farm, it would have been a drain for him to have to continue to pay Aunt Katherine when she was not contributing to the operation and management of the farm. Dad may have needed those funds to hire someone who would help him with the physical labor.

A nuance of the disability trigger is what happens if one of the business owners needs long-term care. Typically, this issue is addressed in the governing document (for instance, the bylaws, operating agreement, or partnership agreement), but most clients I meet with have not addressed that issue yet, so we incorporate that into the business succession plan. If one of the business owners needs long-term care, is the business interest an available asset to help fund the care needed?

I have met with a few clients where in-laws are in business together. Whenever that circumstance presents itself, it is especially advisable to broach the divorce subject as a triggering event. The neighboring farm to my dad's is an operation where the father is in business with his son-in-law. Several years ago, the daughter and son-in-law got a divorce. The question that cropped up was whether the father wanted to stay in business with his ex-son-in-law. As it turns out, the father actually liked his son-in-law, divorced or not, better than his daughter, so he was happy to continue the farming business as it had been all along. Again, similar to the disability example with Aunt Katherine, the circumstances could have been much different. In fact, I would guess there are just as many circumstances like my dad's neighbor that turn out completely different. Whenever I am advising business owners who are in-laws, we always discuss what happens if a divorce occurs. It is always much easier to have the conversation before the actual situation presents itself.

The second part to this question deals with whether the triggering event triggers a mandatory business transition or an optional transition. Obviously, if death is the triggering event, the business transition is mandatory, but if disability and divorce are also triggering events, the question becomes, "Is the transition optional if disability or divorce occurs or is the transition something that has to happen?" If the triggering event allows an optional transition of the business, who has the ability to determine whether the transition will occur? For example, if my dad and Aunt Katherine's business succession plan had included disability as a triggering event, would my dad have had the ability to decide if the business transition occurred upon Aunt Katherine's disability or would Aunt Katherine have had the ability to decide?

If there are multiple business owners, when making a decision about who has the ability to determine if the business transition occurs upon the triggering event, the business owners need to put themselves in the shoes of both individuals: the one who has a disability and the one who does not. Recently, I worked with a business that had two business owners. One of the business owners was at least 25 years older than the second business owner. During the course of creating a business succession plan, I realized that the second (younger) business owner was making all decisions under the assumption that he would be the surviving business owner. I had to pause our discussions and remind the second (younger) business owner that the first (older) business owner could be the surviving business owner, so he should consider how he would want the buy-sell structured for his family if the first (older) business owner was the surviving owner. Once we had that discussion, the whole atmosphere of the meeting changed, and as a result, we had to overhaul the buy-sell agreement and start from scratch.

Question #6: What assets does the business own?

This is my favorite question to ask during a business succession plan meeting because, in my experience, it is such a game changer. I can guarantee that if I am meeting with business owners to discuss business succession planning and their goals for their business succession plan, at least one business owner tells me that one of their major goals is to minimize tax during the business transition, and rightfully so. Business owners are very intelligent individuals; they wouldn't have been successful otherwise, but sometimes they come into our office with tunnel vision. They see one particular type of tax and are so focused on that tax that they miss the orange flag alerting them to other taxes that are sometimes more costly.

If I had been advising my dad and Aunt Katherine on their business succession plan, I would have listened to my dad's concern about federal estate tax and inheritance tax, but I also would have pointed out the orange flag that is capital gains tax. Unfortunately for my dad, from a farming perspective, he has four daughters (although he loves that he has four daughters in all other areas of his life). One is a daycare teacher, one is a nurse, one is an engineer, and one is an attorney, and none of us are overly helpful with the farming. (Sure, I can drive his big Kubota tracker in an open field, but I wouldn't want to have to drive through the barnyard with the hay bales speared on the front of it.) Consequently, if my dad would ever decide he wants to sell the farm, he would have to recognize a huge amount of capital gains. I would have encouraged my dad to stop focusing so heavily on federal estate and inheritance tax, and instead consider the fact that if he pays some tax, then he may be avoiding a much more expensive tax.

When creating a business succession plan, make sure to really look at the assets that the business owns because how the business is transitioned and the method used to facilitate the transfer may depend on what type of assets the business owns.

Before my third year of law school, my roommate and I moved from one apartment building to another. I tried to make the move myself. What a mistake! Remember, I said I don't have spacimization. It was a disaster, and finally my dad took pity on us and drove the five hours to my law school and helped us finish the move (He is a wonderful dad!). I learned that I will never, ever, ever move anywhere without my dad, Krista, or someone possessing the spacimization talent. When I bought my first house in May 2010, I made sure I subtly informed my dad when the closing would be. Okay, I practically circled the date on his calendar with a red marker.

I attended the closing on a Thursday afternoon, and by the time I drove from the closing location to my new house, my dad was waiting in my driveway with his trailer. He had packed up all of my stuff from he and mom's house in two hours, drove the two hours to my new house, and was ready to unload it. Talk about spacimization. Fresh out of law school, I didn't have anything monetarily valuable, but I had one item of sentimental value. My mom had given me the kitchen table that my grandfather had built, and we had eaten at growing up. My dad had carefully packed his trailer to make sure that the table made the move with the least about of scratches as possible. I was so grateful.

I think of my moving stories and spacimization every time I meet with clients to design their business succession plan. I make sure to convey to clients that if this business is a treasured asset then we need to properly package it so it transitions to the future generations in one piece with minimal scratching. I always start with those six basic questions and then follow the road where it takes me, and although I am the worst vehicle packer around and you probably wouldn't want me to help you pack anything for a move, I can take those six questions and use them to wrap your business in plenty of blankets surrounded by lots of pillows to ensure that we are successfully transitioning your business to future generations.

For more information, visit the website of

Steinbacher, Stahl, Goodall & Yurchak

at **www.paeldercounsel.com**

EVERY PARENT WANTS WHAT IS
BEST FOR THEIR CHILDREN

CHAPTER 9

ENDLESS LOVE: PLANNING FOR AN ADULT CHILD WHO HAS SPECIAL NEEDS

Karol A. Bisbee, R.N., Esquire
Accredited Attorney by the Veterans Administration and
Licensed in Massachusetts and New Hampshire

§ 9.1.
JAMIE'S STORY

When Tim, who was 50 years old, walked into my office, the first thing he talked about was Jamie who was 15 at the time. Jamie lived at home with Tim, but it was getting difficult for Tim to care for Jamie who was much bigger than Tim. Eventually Tim had to place Jamie in a residential facility for the developmentally disabled. Tim took Jamie home every weekend and on all the holidays. He went to visit Jamie during the week whenever he could. Jamie had minimal verbal responses and developmentally was like a three-year-old. He needed total care. Tim was a strong advocate for Jamie in obtaining education and services for Jamie. At the age of 18, Tim obtained guardianship of Jamie's person and estate.

At the time of writing this book, Jamie is 24. Tim is divorced, and his own health is precarious, but his first concern is that Jamie will always be provided for. Although Tim has several brothers and sisters, there are really only two that he can count on to provide some support for Jamie when Tim passes away.

Tim was very knowledgeable about Jamie's benefits when he was a minor child under the age of 18 and about what would create problems after Jamie turned 18. However, before becoming educated, Tim thought he had been doing the right thing for Jamie by saving money in his name for several years. Jamie already had $30,000 in his name when Tim first came to see me. The first thing I did for them was create a first party d4A supplemental needs trust for Jamie. Jamie could not have more than $2,000 in his name without jeopardizing important public benefits and even his residential placement. From that point on, Tim made sure he asked lots of questions before he did anything with money in regard to Jamie.

One thing he needed to know was what Jamie's money could be used for and what it could not be used for. Over the years, he had an accessible van that needed to be repaired, and he used some of Jamie's money. He wanted to take Jamie to Disneyland, and he used the trust money. Jamie's medical issues have landed him in the hospital many times, and his life expectancy is unclear. Tim rarely takes at face value advice he is given without verifying it from several sources. After his mistake with saving money in Jamie's name, he wanted to be sure nothing would happen that would jeopardize Jamie's health care and living situation. Tim is very worried about what will happen to Jamie after he passes away. Given his own health issues, this weighs heavily on his mind.

Once Jamie's trust was established, Tim then created his own estate plan and a third party trust for Jamie. He also started keeping a journal so whoever needed to care and advocate for Jamie down the road would have a better understanding of Jamie's idiosyncrasies. Tim hopes this journal will help future caretakers understand what Jamie's form of language means, what he likes and dislikes, what upsets him or makes him angry, and what makes him happy. The journal includes a list of family members, doctors, other health-care professionals, Jamie's medical history, his medications, his daily routine, and everything that Tim could think of that will help whoever is caring for Jamie when Tim is no longer able to. A smooth transition is very important to Tim.

§ 9.2.
CHARLIE'S STORY

Anna arrived at my office with her two sons, Charlie and Matt, along with Matt's wife, Irene. Anna is a mild-mannered woman of 80, and Charlie is her 55-year-old son who has developmental disabilities. Matt and his wife are both healthy adults. The family wanted to make sure that they had their planning done properly to ensure that Charlie is taken care of after Anna is gone.

Charlie is a delightful man, and both his mom and his brother say he has great social skills. He has been working full-time for the past 25 years in a government agency as a custodian. His mom gets him up every day at 4:30 in the morning and helps him get ready for work. He takes a bus to his job. He says the thing he likes most about his job is the people. Charlie will receive a pension, retirement benefits, and good health insurance when he retires. He is very proud of himself because he was able to purchase a one-third interest in a condominium with his own money. The condominium is held jointly with his mother and his brother. He lives there with his mother, who helps him manage his money. He has some significant assets in the bank. Matt and Irene live in the same condominium complex as his mother and Charlie.

Charlie cannot read or write, and he is unable to make change or manage money on his own. When asked who he trusts, he is able to respond that he trusts his mother, and if his mom is not around, then his brother. He enjoys watching car racing, and when there is a race at the local track, he always goes. Everyone at the local races knows him and keeps an eye out for him during the events, and they even announce when he is in the stands. He loves to make model cars, and he uses his money to buy books with pictures in them. Charlie told me, "I have lots of books," with a big smile during our first meeting. When he is done with a book and it is not one he wants to keep, he donates it to friends and family.

Anna never obtained guardianship of Charlie as an adult. While he can answer simple questions, complex questions leave him silent and then "guessing" at an answer. He tears up easily when the discussion turns to the passing of his dad. It was clear from his responses to questions that he could execute a durable power of attorney, health care proxy, HIPAA authorization, and living will. Anna has a will in place and is leaving everything to Matt who will then take care of Charlie if Charlie needs anything.

§ 9.3.
PAUL'S STORY

Eileen came in with her son David with the very definite plan that she wanted a special needs trust for her son Paul. She thought that would be all she needed. Paul was 30 years old at the time and had a diagnosis of bipolar disorder. He is not able to hold a job. Eileen is very involved with NAMI (National Alliance on Mental Illness), and she also communicates with the Bipolar Disorder Advocacy Resource Center (ARC), trying to find solutions for Paul's barriers due to his diagnosis. The lack of assistance available for someone with a bipolar disorder is very frustrating for Eileen.

A mental health diagnosis can be one of the most difficult disabilities to deal with because many times the individual appears like someone without a disability, and society does not see a person with this type of diagnosis as disabled. Resources for people with mental health conditions have been very sparse over the years. After working with Eileen and her son David, who questioned every single recommendation I made, she finally agreed to work with a team that is experienced working with families of people with disabilities, including a financial advisor, to determine what Paul's long-term needs for financial support might be.

Eileen has a significant amount of assets, but she actually believed that she did not have much money before she worked with our team. Paul currently lives independently in a different town and is often angry with Eileen. Eileen often gives Paul $20, and since he likes computers, she recently gave him a gift card to a computer store so he could obtain the things he wants or needs for his computer system. Paul lives in subsidized housing, and he is receiving Social Security income benefits and Medicaid. Paul is often noncompliant with his medical regimen. David and Paul get along well for the most part. After working with the financial advisor, Eileen agreed to set up an entire estate plan for herself and a trust for Paul. She and David agreed that David would be the trustee.

§ 9.4.
PULLING IT TOGETHER

These stories reflect a small cross section of the families who have an adult loved one with a disability and who themselves are also in their second half of life. Sometimes people come into us with no idea of what they need as far as legal planning, but they have an overwhelming concern and worry about who will care for their loved one who is disabled when they are gone. This is what keeps them up at night. This concern is what always comes out in the meetings.

Whether as a factual statement or an emotional declaration, they want to make sure that their child will have someone to care for them and that the appropriate documents are in place to protect the child from losing eligibility for public benefits, especially housing and health care.

The parents are always motivated by love and concern. They are not looking specifically to "save money" or "preserve assets" except to the extent that to do so will result in a higher quality of life for their child. For years, I see parents that have protected and advocated for their child; they have gone through the ups and downs, the hills and valleys, the joys and depressions that come with having a child with special needs. They have procrastinated and put off things till tomorrow, but now that they are entering their twilight – the reality has come home to them that tomorrow could be just around the corner. They know that they need to have all their ducks in a row with plans in place for someone to take up the torch and keep their child, who is living with a disability, safe. They seek the peace of mind in knowing they have done all they can do.

§ 9.5.
THINGS TO CONSIDER WHEN PLANNING FOR AN ADULT CHILD WHO HAS A DISABILITY

In most states, once a child reaches the age of 18, they are considered an adult. At this time, they are their own legal person. It doesn't matter if they have a severe disability; the law presumes they are competent until proven in court that they are not. If planning has not been done, parents no longer have the right to make decisions of any kind on behalf of their child who has a disability. This includes both medical and financial decisions. The parent cannot continue to sign documents or make banking decisions without the legal authority to do so, thus planning becomes very important. Some things to think about include the following:

- Consider whether life insurance is an important part of the plan. It is time to determine what your child's financial needs will be when you are not around.

- Will your child be able to support themself at all and to what extent? Evaluate the availability of any support services and the cost of those services.

- If you had previously set up a revocable or testamentary trust, now is a good time to reexamine the terms to see if they are still appropriate.

- Visit an elder care and special needs planning attorney to help you determine what your child's financial and legal needs are when you are no longer here.

- Is a guardianship necessary? Has it already been put into place? What alternatives to a guardianship may be available?

§ 9.6.
PLANNING FOR A PARENT'S LATER YEARS

One of the most important considerations as you age is preparing your child who has a disability for the fact that one day you will die. There are some important steps that, if not already put into place, need to be carried out now:

- Name a coguardian and/or cotrustee now to avoid a gap where there is no one to make decisions for your child if you suffer a sudden illness or die unexpectedly. Plan now for the possibility that you will have an unexpected change in your health. This will avoid anxiety for your child.

- Have backups to those who have agreed to take over if you can no longer serve as the advocate for your loved one. Name these successor(s) in your will.

- Review and update your will every three to five years or when there has been a change in circumstance with those you have named in your will.

- Now is the time to also review all of your plans with respect to your child's future, such as where s/he will live and whether s/he will be able to continue on with his or her routine if you are not around.

- Prepare a letter of intent to guide the trustee, guardian, family, and caregivers. A letter of intent covers such things as the family history, medical history, housing, education, religion, values, recreation and activity likes, food likes and dislikes, daily routine, what your child can and cannot do, your child's triggers for various emotions or behaviors, what is calming, and what is stressful. A template can be downloaded for free from www.planningandprotecting. com.

- It is time to come up with a specific plan to address how you will distribute your assets. Will there be an inheritance, and will it affect your child's public benefits? What share of your estate should your child who is disabled receive over your other children, and will that cause problems among your children?

§ 9.7.
LEARNING THE TRUST LINGO

Where do I start? What do I do? Your first steps in planning for your child who has a disability may be with your trusted financial advisor or with an attorney who practices in the area of special needs planning. These are the questions for which you seek advice and direction. Special needs planning for a senior parent with an adult child who has a disability is more than a trust. It's not just about the documents. So let's start with a discussion about some of the terms to become familiar with.

So you think you want a trust and have heard that you need a special needs trust in particular, but you have also heard about a supplemental needs trust. Is there any difference between them? No, the terms are interchangeable. Supplemental often refers to the special language found in the trust, which refers to the trust assets being used to supplement the benefits provided by governmental programs such as Social Security, Social Security Income, and Medicaid. The idea is to supplement but not replace the benefits that may be available to the beneficiary who has a disability. Special need often refers to the purpose of the trust to provide for a person who has "special needs." Both terms are now used interchangeably.

There are several types of trusts: A trust may be self-settled or third party. It may be testamentary or inter vivos, and it may be revocable or irrevocable. There are also pooled trusts.

A self-settled trust holds the funds belonging to the individual who has a disability. These trusts may only be created by a parent, grandparent, legal guardian, or the court. In many states, the individual for whom the trust is established must be under the age of 65 when this trust is created. A self-settled trust may hold assets that the individual accumulated through gifts from family and friends; frequently it is funded from an inheritance or the proceeds of a lawsuit. Trust law requires that any assets remaining in the trust at the death of the individual who has a disability be paid back to the state to reimburse Medicaid for the payments it made on behalf of the individual. After Medicaid is paid back, if there are any funds left, they can go wherever the trust provisions direct.

A third-party trust is established with the funds of someone other than the individual who has a disability, for example a parent, grandparent, or friend. The parents might create this trust to be funded upon their death with an inheritance in cash, life insurance, or other assets. This trust can also accept gifts made by others for the benefit of the individual with a disability. This trust does not have an age restriction. More importantly, this trust does not require a pay-back provision when the individual who has a disability dies. At the individual's death, the assets remaining in trust can go wherever the person who created the trust directs.

An inter vivos trust is one that is established during the life of the person creating the trust. This trust could be named in another person's will if he or she wanted to leave something for the individual who has a disability. A testamentary trust does not come into being until someone dies; therefore, the terms are found in someone's will, and it does not contain any assets until the person creating it dies.

An irrevocable trust is one that some part of it cannot be changed. Self-settled trusts can be irrevocable trusts.

A revocable trust is one that can be changed or amended anytime. A third-party trust is usually revocable though it can also be irrevocable if it is funded immediately.

A pooled trust is administered by a nonprofit organization that holds or "pools" the money from many enrolled individuals who have disabilities. The organization generally understands the eligibility rules for the various government programs and manages and disburses the funds in a way that will not disqualify the individual from public benefits. Oftentimes a pooled trust is used when an appropriate individual cannot be found to serve as trustee or the funds are too small for a bank to manage. This trust can be set up by the individual himself, the parent, the guardian, a court, or the grandparent.

§ 9.8.
WHO SHOULD BE THE TRUSTEE

One of the most difficult discussions is about who should be the trustee. There is a strong preference among professionals to appoint a corporate trustee because a special needs trust is complex. Corporate trustees also have insurance that can cover any mistakes they might make affecting government benefit eligibility. Families will often want to name a family member, usually a sibling. A family member who makes a mistake because he or she didn't know the rules will likely not have the money available to return. When a trustee does not know the rules regarding administration and eligibility for public benefits, problems will occur. Families are almost always concerned with the cost of a professional trustee. However, the costs associated with mismanagement by a family trustee can be much more costly.

Also a trust will last through a beneficiary's lifetime, which would be 25 or 30 more years, so flexibility is important. A corporate trustee may be more permanent and provide consistency of administration for an individual who is expected to outlive their parents and likely many other loved ones.

When the trust will only hold a small amount of funds, a trustee can be named with a cotrustee. A family trustee is very common in this instance. Also, families sometimes get together and act as trustees for each other when there is no appropriate family member available and the amounts are small.

§ 9.9.
HOUSING

Housing is always one of the things at the top of every parent's mind. They are concerned about where their child with a disability will live when they are no longer around and how will the cost be paid. Housing options may include living with another family member, living in a residential or institutional facility, Section 8 housing, low-income housing, purchasing a house through a trust, or entering into a group housing arrangement with other families who have children of similar circumstances.

Housing options depend a lot on the severity and type of the person's disability and the person's personality.

§ 9.10.
GUARDIANSHIP AND ALTERNATIVES
TO GUARDIANSHIP

Implementing a guardianship should not be taken lightly. In some states, a guardianship will apply to both health and financial decisions. In other states, the process is bifurcated and a guardian-ship only applies to decisions about the person, for example medical decision making. A conservatorship would be required if a person needed to make decisions about the estate, in other words, the financial aspects of a person's life. Either way a person's rights have been taken away and someone else steps into the person's shoes for making health and/or financial decisions as well as many other life decisions. It is a legal process that requires the involvement of a court to make a determination that a person is incompetent. Each state has its own laws. Many individuals who have developmental or intellectual disabilities can manage their own affairs with some assistance. They may only need a limited guardianship if they need one at all. A guardianship needs to be implemented on an individual basis according to a person's needs. Many times a guardianship may only be necessary when there are behavioral issues that will result in a person revoking more informal alternatives. Another reason for obtaining a conservatorship is to protect the person from those who would prey on the financial status of the person who has a disability. Some other reasons for obtaining a guardianship or conservatorship are:

- When there is not a clear understanding of the individual's ability to consent to treatment or services. Unfortunately, it is often a medical provider's concern over liability as to whether the person has the capacity to provide informed consent that is the issue.

- Again, with health providers, there is a concern over releasing records and information without a clear grant of authority under HIPAA, and if there is a concern of capacity to grant that consent, they will request a guardianship.

§ 9.11.
ALTERNATIVES TO GUARDIANSHIP FOR AN ADULT CHILD WHO HAS DISABILITIES

There are several less restrictive options available as an alternative to a guardianship of the estate or a conservatorship. A representative payee may be appointed to deal with Social Security payments, government, or military payments. This is one way to limit the risk of financial exploitation when a person is not able to manage his or her own money. The Social Security Administration will require regular accounting, and the person is liable if the money is not managed properly. Joint ownership of property is another way to make sure that taxes, insurance, and other real estate ownership issues are taken care of. However, there is always a risk in joint ownership. For example, the healthy child's creditors could claim an interest in the property, and the property could be subject to divorce proceedings. Joint bank accounts are often set up. Again, there are the same issues as with joint property ownership, but it can also be a simple way to pay bills automatically and prevent excessive spending of the money. A trust account is also a good alternative.

Executing certain legal documents is another alternative to guardianship or conservatorship. The health care proxy, also referred to as a durable power of attorney for health care, and the living will address the medical treatment that an individual wants or does not want to receive if he or she is unable to speak with the medical professionals or is deemed incapacitated. The execution of this document when a person is competent to make the decision can avoid the necessity of obtaining a guardianship of the person.

The durable power of attorney is a document that names someone else to handle a person's financial affairs. If validly executed, this document will avoid the necessity of obtaining a conservatorship or guardianship of the estate. Because it is durable, it will survive a person's subsequent incapacity.

§ 9.12.
MEETING WITH THE ATTORNEY

As with our stories in the beginning, everyone came to the attorney's office with a worry and a concern about the future of their child who had a disability but without a clear idea of how to get what they needed. The most important thing about crafting a trust is to build in flexibility, and that can't be done without knowing a lot more about the adult child, family dynamics, and financial and social situation. Before you meet with an attorney, sit down and organize yourself and make a list of this information:

- What kind of government benefits is the child receiving and how much?
- What other income is available?
- What is the current financial situation?
- Is the person mentally or physically competent?
- Is the person already under a guardianship/conservatorship and if so what kind?
- What is the person's condition? Is it stable or worsening?
- Will he or she need long-term care?
- What kind of accommodations need to be made?
- What is his or her daily routine?
- Is he or she going to get SSI, SSDI, or long-term disability?

- What are the current sources of support?
- Are you, the parent, ill? What is your health status? Is long-term care imminent?
- What is the family dynamic? Who is available for support in the long term?
- What medicines is the person taking? Who is the doctor?
- Have you, the parent, done your own basic estate planning?

A discussion about special needs planning is often about planning for multiple generations—the parent, the child who has a disability, and other children or grandchildren. Any plan must also address the potential for being taken advantage of, as those who have disabilities are a highly vulnerable population.

§ 9.13.
WRAPPING IT ALL UP

Jamie's story helped to illustrate how easy it is to make a mistake if you don't know the rules about public benefits and the eligibility requirements. The necessity of a trust when dealing with an adult child who has a severe disability was illustrated here, but in this case, it was also the specific trust created for Jamie's money so he would not lose his government benefits. Tim also created a third-party trust, naming a family member as trustee, as the amount was small. The need for a guardianship was clear here because Jamie was going in and out of hospitals, he was never going to be competent to give any consent, and he needed an advocate who could access all of his information and grant consent to treatments. This also shows how a letter of intent will play a very important part in making sure that

Jamie continues to receive consistent care that will not increase his anxiety. In many circumstances, insurance would also be important in planning for Jamie's future needs, but it was not a concern here.

Charlie's story helped to illustrate that not all individuals who have disabilities need public assistance or a guardian. Charlie could execute documents to let others make decisions if necessary, and he had involved family. In this instance, we did create a sole benefit trust in the event Anna needed to go into a nursing home. She could give the funds outright to Charlie since he was not on any benefits and she could avoid a disqualifying transfer for Medicaid, or she could place the funds into a trust for Charlie's benefit, depending on the situation.

Paul's story also helped to illustrate how planning an entire estate was important and the assistance of a team to plan played an important role in moving the process forward.

No matter what the plan, it requires flexibility because it will last a long time, and we never know when the laws will change. In tough economic times, it can become more difficult to qualify for benefits, so alternative sources of funds always need to be explored, and life expectancy must always be considered.

The goal here is to bring the parent peace of mind, because this child the parent has nurtured and cared for with unwavering devotion will have a plan to meet his or her needs and assure that the child receives the care and support the parent wants for him or her when the parent is no longer here to provide for the child. Medical advances allow us all to live longer, so this endless love must reach far into the future.

For more information, visit the website of the

Law Office of Karol Bisbee, P.C.

at **www.bisbeelaws.com**

DON'T GET TAKEN BY PHONE SCAMS

CHAPTER 10

THE FINANCIAL EXPLOITATION OF VULNERABLE SENIORS

Beth Ann R. Lawson, Esquire

Member of the National Association of Elder Law Attorneys
Accredited Attorney by the Veterans Administration

Many American seniors are unwilling participants in an ongoing reality show called, *Who Is Stealing My Nest Egg?* This show may be playing live in a household very near to you[25].

Ellen was sitting in her kitchen when the phone rang. She picked it up, and the voice said, "Grandma, Grandma, this is Ted. I am in trouble. Please help me. I am in England on spring break. Someone stole my wallet. I need $500 to get back home. I can't call Dad. He will be furious. You can't tell him." Ellen was shaken. Ted had been away at college for two years, and she had barely heard from him. She was glad that her grandson trusted her to help.

Ted said he was afraid that the group's bus would leave without him if he couldn't get the money wired in the next 30 minutes. Ellen told him not to worry and wired the $500, saying "Call me when you get the money."

Ellen didn't hear from Ted and, she worried all night. She called her daughter the next morning to tell her that Ted was in trouble in England. Ted's mother told Ellen that Ted was at college. Ellen got Ted's phone number and called him at his dorm. "I'm fine, Gram. What's up?" Ellen told him what had just happened.

§ 10.1. Introduction

§ 10.2. What Is the Financial Exploitation of Seniors?

§ 10.3. Why the Financial Exploitation of Seniors Continues to Succeed

§ 10.4. Who Are the Victims?

§ 10.5. Methods Used to Make Contact with Senior Victims

§ 10.6. Common Financial Scams against Seniors

§ 10.6.1. Telephone Scams

§ 10.6.2. Sweepstakes and Sweetheart Scams

§ 10.6.3. Face-to-Face/Door-to-Door Scams

§ 10.6.4. Home Repair Scams

§ 10.6.5. Predatory Lending Practices

§ 10.7. Legal Planning to Reduce the Financial Exploitation of Seniors

§ 10.8. Practical Family Policies to Prevent the Financial Exploitation of Vulnerable Seniors

§ 10.9. Summary

§ 10.1.
INTRODUCTION

"Fool me once, shame on you. Fool me twice, shame on me." This often-quoted axiom is horribly unjust when applied to seniors who have some form of physical frailty or dementia who become the victims of financial exploitation. "Fool me at all, shame on you" is more appropriate. At risk to "financial exploitation is the fastest rising form of elder abuse,"[26] especially for the millions of American seniors who have dementia or Alzheimer's.

In 2010, the estimated financial loss by victims of elder financial abuse was $2.9 billion[27]. The ongoing estimate is that for every reported incident of senior financial abuse, another four or more incidents go unreported[28]. Described over three decades ago in a Congressional report on aging as a concept "alien to the American Ideal,"[29] senior financial exploitation is now commonplace across all social levels.

With current technology, who, at any age, can fully protect themselves from savvy financial exploiters? Thieves sabotage ATM machines and exploit the multitudes. E-mail exploitation occurs at all ages. If the general public cannot protect itself against scammers, how can fragile seniors fend off financial exploitation from both family and strangers at the most vulnerable time in their lives? Can seniors who refuse to report caregiver exploitation for fear of being abandoned be convinced that the best solution is to report the crime that may result in them being put into a nursing home?

Recent high-profile cases of the financial exploitation of very wealthy seniors by family members involve actor Mickey Rooney and the wealthy socialite author, Brooke Astor. Family embezzlement of the very wealthy is national news, but the daily exploitation of non-celebrities may fail to make it into a police report.

§ 10.2.
WHAT IS THE FINANCIAL
EXPLOITATION OF SENIORS?

Financial abuse of seniors includes the taking of assets, whether illegally or improperly, which belong to the victim. This could include appropriating money, real estate, artwork, jewelry, vehicles, credit, and identities. The definition of this crime continues to evolve among the professional disciplines that are tasked with its prevention.

Seniors often need help managing their finances and paying bills as they age. A senior is at the mercy of the ethics of who they choose to manage their finances. Relatives, caretakers, strangers, and corporate and legal entities are all potential fiscal protectors or predators.

Differing tactics are employed by scammers to take assets from a senior. Force, psychology, undue influence, intimidation, and fraud are common methods. Force is used in stealing the purses of elderly women, breaking into seniors' homes, and exercising different forms of physical abuse to separate fragile seniors from their money or property. Emotional abuse includes threats, abandonment, isolating the senior from companionship, and creating dependence upon the exploiter. Fraud, scams, and schemes involve putting a senior into a state of urgent, isolated decision making to buy services that are over-priced, unnecessary, or nonexistent. Corporate financial exploitation occurs through the abuse of officially appointed positions such as guardianships, conservatorships, and representative payees.

Financial exploitation of seniors is devastating because the crime is directed at an age group without the time or capability to restore depleted funds. It presents a bitter scenario for seniors who understand that they are being victimized, but have limited alternatives for care. A senior may choose not to report a fiscal abuse to avoid being abandoned by the exploiter.

§ 10.3.
WHY FINANCIAL EXPLOITATION CONTINUES TO SUCCEED

Betty's husband passed away. Betty's children installed a home security system to protect their mom from crime. Betty set the alarm each night, but not during the day.

Betty's drug addict grandson broke into her home when she was out. The alarm was not on. He used Betty's Social Security number to open credit accounts for cash. When Betty discovered the theft, she was ashamed that she had left the security system off. Her daughter begged her not to call the police on her son. Not wanting to lose her daughter's companionship, Betty remained silent and assumed the debt. Her daughter promised that the grandson would pay her back at some time.

The natural effects of aging make seniors prime targets for fiscal abuse. Aging can include the natural slowing of information processing, dementia, hearing loss, cognitive impairment, health issues, drug interactions, loss of a spouse, isolation, loss of driving skills, physical frailties, and side effects from the treatments for various diseases. Seniors often have assets, which also make them attractive targets.

The exploitation of seniors is underprosecuted, making it attractive to predators. To prosecute a crime, a crime has to be reported.

Dementia may erase any memory of an abuse. Seniors may forget details needed as evidence. Age and the passage of time are not conducive to a senior being a strong witness in a court of law, and the senior may pass away before trial.

When a fiscal predator is a caregiver who threatens physical harm or placement in a nursing home, a powerful incentive exists for seniors with or without dementia to forget about the abuse.

Seniors who report abuse can face family and public criticism for "letting the abuse happen." Seniors find their independence assaulted as the family "takes over." That the senior was a victim of a professionally organized attack often gets lost in the heat of fixing the problem. Rather than lose control over their affairs, seniors may hide an abuse. Predators count on this silence.

§ 10.4.
WHO ARE THE VICTIMS?

Seniors are the victims, and their numbers are exploding. In a study of 5,777 older adults, 5.2 percent of Americans age 60 and older had already been the victim of recent financial exploitation by a family member, while 6.5 percent were targets of a non-family member[30]. Women are nearly twice as likely to be victims as men[31]. Most victims are between the ages of 80 and 89[32].

The number of seniors who have Alzheimer's disease is estimated at 5.1 million Americans. Currently, one out of eight people age 65 and over has Alzheimer's disease, and nearly one out of two Americans over age 85 suffer from it. By 2050, Americans 65 and older who have Alzheimer's disease will number 13.5 million.

As seniors stop driving or become homebound and less involved with community groups, social isolation begins. This is a window of opportunity for scammers. A homebound senior may begin to welcome any opportunity for social interaction, including phone sales representatives, door-to-door salesmen, and unknown neighbors. A victim can become a predator's strongest ally because the senior needs the continued attention.

Major life changes open a senior to disorientation and create a window of opportunity for someone to "take over." Losing a spouse, relocating, experiencing an extended hospital stay, or experiencing the onset of dementia are life changing at any age. Confusion provides fertile opportunities for an exploiter's access to a senior's money.

§ 10.5.
METHODS USED TO MAKE
CONTACT WITH SENIORS

Family members who financially abuse their senior relatives may do so with the innocent assistance of the victim. Seniors add relative's names to financial accounts to help with bill paying. Names are added to house and car titles. Relatives are named as financial powers of attorney and are able to move money around at will. An ill-chosen agent may topple the senior's financial security.

Financial predators may contact victims through telephone solicitations, face-to-face/door-to-door meetings, marketing mailers, and the Internet. Technology provides unmonitored and ongoing access to seniors in their homes. Through the Internet, unwary seniors can invite predators into their worlds and bank accounts with one keystroke, solving a scammer's problem of how to contact new victims.

§ 10.6.
COMMON SCAMS USED TO EXPLOIT SENIORS

Susan, a 90-year-old widow, lives alone. She drives short distances and pays her own bills. Her daughter, Amy, lives several hours away and has suspected that her mother has entered the early stages of undiagnosed Alzheimer's.

Susan called Amy to say she had allowed two men to enter her house to make emergency repairs for $5,000. The men came to her door to tell her that there was dangerous mold outside of her house and that it was probably in the attic. The men wanted cash to start work right away before the house collapsed. Susan went to the bank. The men hosed down the outside of the house, hammered a board up in the attic, and left with the cash. Susan was proud of her fast work in saving her home. Amy was grateful that the only loss to her mother was money and pride.

Technology has opened up a new world of social contact for homebound seniors. E-mailing friends and family has reinvigorated many lives. Yet the Internet also poses a world of danger. Educating seniors on the positive and negative aspects of Internet safety should be a priority in preventing new fiscal abuse.

The following is an abbreviated list of financial exploitation scams adapted from a comprehensive report offered by the North Carolina Attorney General's Office. The North Carolina report is an excellent example of government action to educate senior groups on self-protection.

§ 10.6.1.
Telephone Scams

1. **Grandparent Scams**: Scammer poses as grandchild in an emergency situation in need of money for safety, but the grandparent/senior must not tell the parents.

2. **Prize Check Scam**: "You Have Won" checks from overseas where you have to wire back substantial money to cover taxes and to get your winnings, which do not exist.

3. **Counterfeit Checks from Phony Lottery and Sweepstakes Companies**: These require money to be wired immediately after you receive and deposit a phony check in order to get the million-dollar winnings, which do not exist. You lose the wired money.

4. **Identity Theft Insurance**: Pay us hundreds of dollars, and give us all your private information so we can protect you from scams. Federal law is already in place, which protects people from identity theft and misuse of credit card numbers.

5. **Recovered Assets**: We have located money or property belonging to you. Call a toll-free number, and then provide a Social Security number, bank account, and mother's maiden name to allow the assets to be returned. Bank accounts are then electronically debited.

6. **Medicare Discount Drug Cards**: Call comes with offer of this card, and you give your bank account number to allow for a debit for the card. If a card exists, it may not apply to your area or there may not be a card. The scammer withdraws funds from your account.

7. **Your Phone/Power/Gas Service**: A call comes saying you are past due on payments, and your services will be

immediately disconnected if you do not pay immediately over the phone with a credit card or with your bank account number. Withdrawals are made.

8. **Death Threats**: After a first scam, the scammer demands more money and threatens to kill you or harm your family. The caller is usually based overseas with no intention to contact you further.

§ 10.6.2.
Sweepstakes and Sweetheart Scams

9. **You May Already Be a Winner!** Buy this to be eligible for the grand prize.

10. **Sweetheart Scam**: Individual professes love or affection for the lonely senior and then gains control over the estate and gets appointed as the agent under a power of attorney and a beneficiary in the senior's will.

11. **Overseas Money Scams**: We have a lot of money to transfer and will pay you a 25 percent commission to allow us to put it in your bank account. Give us your bank number and pay us several thousand dollars to bribe a foreign official into releasing the money into your account.

12. **Your Distant Relative Has Died in Our Country:** He left you a lot of money, which the government is going to take. Pay us to get the money for you. There is not really an estate.

§ 10.6.3.
Face-to-Face/Door-to-Door Scams

13. **Distraction Theft**: One thief distracts the victim while the other steals. This scam is also used to inspect a house for a future robbery. This technique is used internationally against tourists.

14. **Phony Police Detectives**: They search your house for valuables and stake it out or steal as they go.

15. **Woman in Distress at the Front Door**: Normally two women together, and while one holds your attention, the other goes to the bathroom and steals items along the way.

16. **Sound-Alike Charities and Law Enforcement Groups**: They solicit donations.

§ 10.6.4.
Home Repair Scams

17. **Your Chimney Is Falling Down**: A useless fix is applied to a perfectly good chimney.

18. **My Leg Went through Your Roof**: Gutter repairman says you need a new roof when you don't.

19. **Toilet Bowl Scams**: Repair person puts water around the toilet and tells you it has to be replaced at a significant cost

20. **Your House Does Not Meet Code.** We can fix it before the city inspector condemns it.

21. **Frozen Pipe Scams**: Pipes under the house are "frozen" (they aren't) and will explode and ruin the structure if they are not replaced before they thaw.

§ 10.6.5.
Predatory Lending Practices

22. Predatory Lending Practices: Include exorbitant interest rates, balloon payments, and fraudulent reverse mortgages, which strip the home's equity.

Additional materials on this topic may be obtained by contacting John Bison at the North Carolina Attorney General's office, this author, your state's local Attorney General's office, Consumer Protection agencies, and AARP. This information should be shared with seniors, their caregivers, and their families.

§ 10.7.
LEGAL PLANNING TO REDUCE THE FINANCIAL EXPLOITATION OF SENIORS

Mr. M, aged 88, lost his wife last year. His children hired a live-in caregiver. Mr. M's caregiver brings Mr. M to his lawyer. Mr. M tells his lawyer that he wants to marry the 40-year-old caregiver. He wants to deed his house into the caregiver's name immediately as a wedding gift. They will get married, and Mr. M will not have to go to a nursing home.

The lawyer explains the dangers of this action to Mr. M who appears somewhat disoriented and asks if Mr. M has discussed this with his family. He says no but refuses to let the lawyer contact his family. When the caregiver discovers that the lawyer has refused to do the deed until Mr. M talks to his family and doctor, she says, "Let's go. I know a better attorney." The probability is that she did find an attorney to draft the deed who is not familiar with senior issues and exploitation.

Legal protection begins with voluntary legal planning while an individual has the mental capacity to execute legal documents. It then moves along the full spectrum to involuntary court-ordered legal protection if needed. Lawyers, doctors, and financial planners should have client discussions about the need for financial and medical legal protection early in their relationship with a senior. A senior without legal documents, such as powers of attorney, and who then develops dementia may become an unwilling participant in civil court proceedings where a court has to assign control of the senior's person and assets to someone else.

Creating legal protection does not rest in a single document. It is a system. It begins with identifying assets and creating the best methods of protection. Using direct deposit for checks may or may not be a good measure of protection. Jointly titling property or accounts can bring protection or provide legal access to a predator. Assigning a representative payee may be helpful. It depends on the needs of the senior. Working with a legal professional to design a system of protection that is monitored is an important defense to being financially exploited.

Helping seniors identify someone to act as their legal protector during incapacity is important. In legal documents such as powers of attorney, wills, and trusts, seniors define the powers they wish for a named person(s) to exercise on their behalf should they become incapacitated. Too many people name their children in order of age without considering their children's strengths, financial situations, religious beliefs about end-of-life issues, availability, and desire to act as a legal representative. The senior should consider whether a non-relative would be a more effective choice. Who will keep the senior's interests a priority? A senior's most important task is to select the right agent for the senior's future protection.

Powers of attorney are lynchpins in legal fiscal protection. Using a power of attorney, a senior can maintain control until he or she is mentally unable to do so. With clearly defined powers and direction, an agent under a financial durable power of attorney can follow the wishes of the senior where feasible and act in the best interests of the senior at all times. The same rules apply for medical powers of attorney and living wills by means of which the agent may have to make a life-ending decision for a senior.

Some seniors worry that one child will be angry if a better-suited child is named as the agent. But the parent lists the lesser-suited child to "keep the peace." The result will not promote family peace when the ill-suited child takes charge of the parent's welfare. Having this conversation is an important part of legal planning because legal protection is only as good as the appointed agent. This same conversation should occur for appointing a trustee of a trust, naming a future guardian and conservator, or stating a preference as to who should act as a representative payee.

Without legal documents in place, a court of law may have to intervene. Civil courts appoint guardians and conservators for the incapacitated. If someone successfully petitions a court for appointment as a conservator or guardian, the court has legally determined that the individual has diminished capacity. The court transfers the incapacitated person's legal right to make his or her own decisions to another individual or agency. The court may also issue orders of protection when a senior is found to be under undue influence or, as in some cases, imprisoned or fully isolated in his or her home by an exploiter. Again preplanning to name designated people to be named as a guardian or conservator allows the judge to follow the senior's wishes.

§ 10.7.
PRACTICAL FAMILY POLICIES TO PREVENT THE FINANCIAL EXPLOITATION OF VULNERABLE SENIORS

Educating seniors and their families on fiscal abuse prevention and reporting must become a national cooperative effort. Public knowledge of the schemes used to exploit seniors will put a spotlight on an activity that thrives in secrecy.

The following practical prevention actions are beginning steps to safety:

1. Educate! Educate seniors, professionals, and the public on senior financial exploitation, its impact, and its cost. Publicize information on new scams. Maintain a community scam hotline.

2. Eliminate criticism and the after-abuse of a senior victimized by a financial scammer. Applaud seniors for reporting financial abuse to the police. Tell everyone. Tell family, friends, church, reporters, neighbors, and social groups. Be a hero and save the next victim from falling prey to the same scam.

3. If there is an offer where acceptance must be immediate or it is lost, say goodbye to the "opportunity" and say hello to the safety of your nest egg.

4. Caller ID is a valuable tool in stopping scammer calls. Do not accept calls from unknown numbers. Do not conduct business over the phone unless you called first. Do not deal with lenders by phone unless you called them first.

5. DO NOT give out your Social Security number, bank numbers, or credit card numbers over the phone.

6. If you did not call for a repair, do not allow service technicians to enter your home. There should be an appointed time for their arrival, and check the technician's ID before letting them in your home.

7. Understand a contract before signing. Have an attorney review it. Keep the paperwork. You need it to prove what was agreed to. Get home repair contracts in writing regardless of the scope of work. Check references with the Better Business Bureau. People have three days to cancel a contract, but need to cancel in writing.

8. Never wire money. Send a check, which you can cancel if needed.

9. Shred all paper with identifying information before you put it in the trash. Trash cans are treasure troves for identity thieves.

§ 10.8.
SUMMARY

The prevention, detection, and prosecution of senior financial abusers is a massive undertaking. It is bigger than the resources of any single government agency. Cooperative efforts by government agencies, such as adult protective services and social services along with the legal community, the legislature, medical professionals, financial planners, investment companies, the banking industry, advocate volunteer groups, and seniors themselves will be needed in a successful prevention of abuse. Getting these disciplines to cooperate will not be without resistance. Client confidences, ethics, and privacy protection laws are initial hurdles to change; however, discussion is occurring in these areas on a national basis.

Frank Abagnale, a fraud expert and the subject of the movie *Catch Me If You Can*, said of financial fraud against the elderly, "I have always believed that the government should take the lead in education to combat this horrendous crime… If you educate and explain to people their risks, in most cases they are smart enough to take that information and reduce their risks. I believe education is the only approach to help eliminate elder fraud." An expert on exploitation has spoken.

For more information, visit the website of

Carrell Blanton Ferris, Attorneys at Law

www.carrellblanton.com

[25] The following image of the thief comes from Milestones e-news Marcia Z. Siegal, *Get wise to scams!*, http://www.pcacares.org/Milestones_Main_Web_Details. aspx?story=563P4G22K38

[26] Marcia Z. Siegal, *Get wise to scams!*, http://www.pcacares.org/Milestones_Main_ Web_Details.aspx?story=563P4G22K38 (citing Joe Snyder, director of older adult protective serves at Philadelphia Corporation for Aging).

[27] The MetLife Study of Elder Financial Abuse, p. 2 (June 2011), https://www.metlife. com/mmi/research/elder-financial-abuse.html#key%20findings

[28] Marcia Z. Siegal, *Get wise to scams!*, http://www.pcacares.org/Milestones_Main_ Web_Details.aspx?story=563P4G22K38

[29] US Administration on Aging, *Elder Abuse: A Decade of Shame and Inaction*, A report by the Chairman of the Subcommittee on Health and Long-Term Care of the Select Committee on Aging, House of Representatives One Hundred First Congress Second Session, April 1990, Comm. Pub. No. 101-752, p. IX of the Executive Summary of the Report on Aging.

[30] Ron Acierno et al., US Dep't of Justice, National Elder Mistreatment Study (Mar. 2009), https://www.ncjrs.gov/App/Search/SearchResults.aspx?txtKeywordSearch=nation al+elder+mistreatment+study&fromSearch=1

[31] The MetLife Study of Elder Financial Abuse, p. 3 (June 2011), https://www.metlife. com/mmi/research/elder-financial-abuse.html#key%20findings

[32] *Id.*

JOE RECEIVES ANOTHER
RETIREMENT FUND STATEMENT

CHAPTER 11

ACHIEVE A SECURE RETIREMENT...
AVOID FIVE COMMON MISTAKES
OF RETIREMENT PLANNING

Dennis J. Toman,
Certified Elder Law Attorney

Dennis J. Toman, Certified Elder Law Attorney (CELA) by the National Elder Law Foundation; Board Certified Specialist in both Elder Law and Estate Planning by the North Carolina State Bar; and Member of Council of Advanced Practitioners (CAP) by the National Academy of Elder Law Attorneys.

§ 11.1.
BOB AND MARY'S PLAN

Bob and Mary are like many families I help. Bob worked in industry, and Mary taught school. They worked hard, raised a family, contributed to their community, and now they are nearing retirement. Neither of them made a lot of money, but they saved hard, and their savings have grown to include their house (paid for) and substantial retirement savings, although they aren't millionaires. They have some money in retirement plans, including their own IRAs. They have some life insurance, and their investments are in several different types of accounts. They are confused about Social Security, are worried whether they will have enough money for retirement, and wonder whom to trust to help them.

They are looking forward to retirement. Freedom! But that freedom comes at a price: their regular paycheck. They know that their financial future depends on their savings and how they invest now and in the future. With a good plan, they can have peace of mind.

§ 11.2.
YOUR PLAN

Like Bob and Mary, you don't want to make mistakes about your own retirement either. Your situation may be different from theirs, but your questions will be similar. The good news is that you'll get lots of good information and direction from reading this chapter.

Are you near retirement or already retired? Naturally, you wonder, "How can I enjoy a secure retirement, feeling comfortable that I will not outlive my money?"

Some people approach retirement with a sizeable nest egg; others have more modest assets. Some people have been investing their whole lives, while others feel overwhelmed and don't know where to begin.

As an elder law attorney, my clients raise critical questions about a number of key retirement issues. Retirement requires addressing a number of different areas, including legal issues, financial concerns, health care, family relationships, lifestyle, and life purpose.

You've heard the old joke that goes something like this. *A robber pulls a gun on a couple walking, pointing the gun at the husband. The robber shouts, "Your money or your life?" and waits. The husband says nothing, so the robber demands, "Hurry up!" After another long pause the husband says, "Don't rush me, I'm thinking it over!"*

That's funny, especially when Jack Benny told it. But let's switch that around. What if the robber's name is "Retirement," and he asks you, "Your money or your lifestyle?" That isn't as funny. In fact, it's not funny at all. But your choices about money—your income, life savings, and investment decisions—directly affect your lifestyle in retirement.

True, retirement finances are not a level playing field for everyone. Some people near retirement are with little or no savings because of tough economic times or low-paying jobs. Others faced family or health struggles that drained their finances.

For everyone entering retirement this chapter has important information to help you make the right decision about when to start receiving Social Security. If you have a retirement nest egg, however large or small, you'll face not only the decision about when to start Social Security but also how to manage and spend your savings during your lifetime and, hopefully, to someday pass on to your family what's left.

Based on what I've seen with families I've worked with, you'll have a better retirement if you avoid these five common mistakes in retirement planning.

§ 11.3.
MISTAKE #1:
NOT UNDERSTANDING YOUR OPTIONS
FOR STARTING SOCIAL SECURITY

If you've already started receiving Social Security, you can skip to the next section. But if you're nearing age 60 or have delayed applying for Social Security because you're not sure of your options, here is valuable information that could make a tremendous difference for your retirement for many years to come.

§ 11.3.1.
When Should You Start Social Security?

Every baby boomer approaching age 62 wonders, "Should I apply for Social Security as early as possible or wait until later to receive more each month?" Naturally, there is no one right answer. Maximizing your benefits depends on your situation and your overall financial plan. Here's helpful guidance.

§ 11.3.2.
When May You Begin Receiving Benefits?

Full retirement age is 66 for people born from 1943 to 1954. It goes up slightly for later retirees and is age 67 for those born after 1959. You can start receiving benefits at age 62 or wait as long as until age 70. Your monthly check depends on your wage history, your birth date, your spouse's benefits, and how long you wait to request benefits.

§ 11.3.3.
Should You Request Benefits Early or Wait?

Conventional wisdom has been to start right away. And for someone with small savings, poor health, and no plans to work after age 62, you should start early. For everyone else, you should consider delaying Social Security if you expect to live a long time and want to get a bigger check for many years.

Here's an example from the Social Security Administration to give you an idea of what's at stake. Let's say you were born in 1949 and would have a monthly benefit of $1,000 starting at age 66 (full retirement age). If you start benefits at age 62, your monthly benefit would be reduced by 25 percent to $750. If you defer benefits until age 70, your monthly amount would be $1,320 (32 percent more per month than if your benefits started at age 66 and a *whopping 76 percent more* than if you started right away at age 62)[33].

Of course, if you knew how long you were going to live, this would be a simple mathematical calculation. If you live much longer than average, you'll benefit most by delaying Social Security. Your family history can give you some idea of longevity. You also can get a personalized estimate of how long you will live from www.livingto100. com, based on your answers to about 40 health and family questions.

§ 11.3.4.
How Does This Affect Your Spouse?

A married person with little or no earnings history can receive a benefit equal to half of the higher-earning spouse's benefit. For example, if Boomer Dave is married to Boomer Peggy who spent her time as a homemaker rather than working outside the home, she won't have a Social Security earnings record. However, Peggy can apply for a spousal benefit based on one-half of what Dave's amount would be at full retirement (i.e., age 66 for current retirees). Peggy's benefit would be reduced if she applied before age 66. But she shouldn't wait beyond age 66, because her benefit is capped and does not increase if she waits beyond her full retirement of age 66. So for Peggy, she should apply no later than age 66, unless she wants to apply sooner and receive a smaller benefit.

There is a slight catch for Peggy. She cannot receive benefits before Dave files for his retirement. That's a problem if Peggy is age 62 and Dave plans to keep working and delay his benefits until age 70. However, after Dave reaches age 66 (his full retirement age), he could file for and suspend payment of his Social Security until he reaches age 70. That allows Peggy to get her check sooner, while Dave's benefit continues to increase through age 70. Another advantage to this plan is if Dave dies before Peggy, she will get more under her survivor benefit (which is different from the spousal benefit) than if Dave started taking his benefits before age 70.

When both spouses are high earners, the calculation changes. Let's say Peggy had a high-paying career and her maximum benefit is $1,800. After Peggy applies for her benefit, then Dave could apply when he turns 66 but only for his spousal benefit. That would give him his spousal benefit income of $900 per month for several years. Then when Dave turns 70, he'll claim his own benefit (instead of the spousal benefit) and start collecting a check that will be higher than it would have been if he'd claimed it at age 66.

§ 11.3.5.
If You're Divorced or Widowed

You can receive spousal benefits based on your ex-spouse's earnings if you were married for at least ten years and you are currently unmarried. Full benefits are calculated for starting at age 66, but you may apply as early as age 62 with reduced benefits. If you've been divorced from your spouse for at least two years, you don't have to wait until he's applied for his benefits; however, he would have to be at least age 62 and eligible for benefits.

If you're widowed, you can apply for survivor benefits as early as age 60 (or age 50 if you are disabled). The survivor benefit equals 100 percent of your spouse's benefit, but is reduced if you apply before age 66. You can get the higher of your own benefit or your spouse's (but not both).

If you and your spouse both are receiving Social Security, your spouse's benefits stop at his or her death. You can then switch over to survivor's benefits if higher than your own. Here are three key points to understand about this. First, if the deceased spouse waited until age 70 to start receiving benefits, the survivor's benefits will be higher than if he or she had started earlier. Second, there is no "two for one" in Social Security. When one spouse dies, one of the checks will stop. And third, if you remarry before age 60, your survivor benefits will stop (age 50 if you are disabled).

§ 11.3.6.
When Are Social Security Benefits Taxable?

Your Social Security may be taxed depending on your other income. None of your benefits are taxed unless you exceed certain income thresholds. Once your other income, from working or investments, exceeds those thresholds, you could pay tax on 50 percent or 85 percent of your Social Security benefits. That might be another reason to continue working past 66 but delay Social Security until age 70—to reduce taxes while maximizing your Social Security. Similarly, you might delay Social Security until age 70 while you start pension payments or take taxable distributions from IRAs.

§ 11.3.7.
More Help Is Available from the Social Security Administration

Fortunately, there are places to get some help with these calculations, starting at the Social Security Administration's own website, www.socialsecurity.gov. If you are planning on working while drawing Social Security, there is a calculator that shows how working affects your benefits.

§ 11.4.
MISTAKE #2:
NOT FOLLOWING AT LEAST A BASIC FINANCIAL PLAN

Regardless of your finances, you need a financial plan. Not only is it common sense, but many studies about retirement tell us that retirees who are financially prepared feel more satisfied in retirement.

I've observed the importance of having a financial plan in a variety of circumstances. I've met wealthy clients who always worried they didn't have enough money. A financial plan could have reassured them. They could have stopped worrying and relaxed. I've also had married clients who assumed they had plenty of money. They committed to a retirement community. But then one spouse's medical expenses hit them hard and drained their savings, so they were barely able to survive financially. And of course, my clients with limited finances must make decisions to stretch retirement savings based on planning ahead and budgeting carefully.

A survey[34] by the Employee Benefit Research Institute about retirement planning in America revealed a reality gap among American retirees and an overall lack of planning:

- Sixty-two percent of American retirees are confident that they will have enough money to live comfortably throughout retirement.
- In reality, nearly three out of four of those same retirees have less than $100,000 total in savings and investments.
- Among working adults, only 66 percent are actually saving for retirement; of those, the majority have a nest egg of less than $50,000.
- Forty-five percent of American workers simply guess about their retirement needs.

A word of advice for parents who are retired—let your children know something about your plan. Don't let them presume you have plenty of money and no worries when that's not the case. You'll do yourself and your children a favor by having an open discussion about your retirement planning. And who knows? Maybe by sharing this information, your children will see your example and do a better job of their own planning too!

§ 11.5.
MISTAKE #3:
NEVER BECOMING A STUDENT OF YOUR OWN INVESTMENT PLANNING

If someone handed you a box full of oil paints and asked you to paint, how would it look the first time you tried? Probably not very good. Unless you're naturally gifted, you'd have to learn about painting and then practice, practice, practice. It's the same for your retirement financial planning…except that you don't want to practice on your retirement savings.

To be an artist, you need to learn about colors and techniques and then apply the colors based on the result you want. It's the same way with your investment planning. Choose your investments based on what you want in retirement. But before you can do that, you need to know enough about investments to make smart decisions.

You can study investment planning on your own, or you can hire a financial advisor. Even if you're working with a financial advisor, you need to know enough to understand and evaluate his or her recommendations for you. Too many clients have told me that they simply followed financial advice, but later they looked back and felt that they would have made different choices if they had known more about investing.

A word of caution. As a boomer or retiree, you represent an attractive client for financial advisors since you're needing to move from "accumulating" savings for retirement to "producing income" in retirement. Simply being a knowledgeable investor will not protect you unless you stay alert to avoid falling for sales pitches from the wrong advisors.

§ 11.5.1.
Choosing Your Financial Advisor

Choosing the right financial advisor depends on your expertise, comfort level, and needs. Here are some suggestions about how to make this decision.

If you're a "do-it-yourselfer" and want to make your own investment decisions, you can consider a discount broker or buying a no-load mutual fund family. But approach this cautiously. Don't overestimate your abilities or your mistakes can ruin your retirement (and ruin your spouse's retirement too if you're married).

If you're generally comfortable with making your own investment decisions yet would like some suggestions, consider a commissioned advisor such as a registered representative (also called a stockbroker or account executive) or an insurance agent. Many clients have found rewarding relationships with a broker or insurance agent who provides the right financial products and advice, while being paid on a commission arrangement.

However, if you want to have someone else manage and monitor your portfolio for you, you would need a registered investment advisor, either directly if you have enough invested or through a "separately managed account" (or SMA) for smaller accounts.

§ 11.5.2.
Learning about the Four Categories of Financial Advisors

There are four general categories of financial advisors, based on how they are regulated, which license(s) they hold, and the type of services or products they offer[35]. This can be confusing because some advisors and their companies wear multiple hats and many terms are similar.

1. **Registered representatives** are licensed to <u>sell securities</u>. Those with the most comprehensive license (a "Series 7" license) can sell a full range of stocks and bonds, as well as mutual funds and variable annuities. Other registered representatives can only sell mutual funds, variable annuities, and similar products because they have only the "Series 6" license. Both are licensed through the Financial Industry Regulatory Authority (FINRA), which regulates security firms in the United States. They work for "broker-dealers" and often are called stockbrokers, brokers, or account representatives. They can also include someone selling securities in a bank's office. Registered representatives generally are paid through commissions on sales. You can get more information about registered representatives at the FINRA website, at <u>www.finra.org</u>.

2. **Registered investment advisors** (or RIAs) <u>sell investment advice</u>. RIAs are licensed through the federal Securities Exchange Commission (SEC) or the states in which they have clients, depending on the value of their clients' assets. RIAs must act as "fiduciaries" for their clients, meaning that they must avoid self-interest when giving investment advice suitable to clients. RIAs may be paid various ways: a percentage of the value of the assets they manage for clients, an hourly fee, a fixed fee, or a commission on the securities they sell (if the advisor is also a broker-dealer). You can get information about an RIA registered with the SEC, at <u>www.adviserinfo.sec.gov</u>.

3. **Insurance agents** <u>sell life insurance products, fixed annuities, and indexed annuities</u>. They are licensed by their state's insurance commissioner. To sell variable annuities they also must have at least a Series 6 license (see above). Insurance agents are paid commissions based on the particular product sold. You can find out more about how insurance agents are regulated by your state by visiting the website for the National Association of Insurance Commissioners at <u>www.naic.org</u>.

4. **Financial planners** are not regulated or licensed, and they <u>sell financial planning services</u>. They can't sell securities, insurance, or investment advice unless they also hold the appropriate license as discussed above. Other generic titles that don't require licenses include financial analyst, financial consultant, financial planner, investment consultant, and wealth management. Likewise, someone who is a "Certified Financial Planner™" or "Certified Senior Advisor" may or may not be licensed to sell investments or provide investment advice. You would need more information in order to understand that person's credentials.

§ 11.6.
MISTAKE # 4:
UNDERESTIMATING THE LENGTH AND COST OF RETIREMENT

When considering your retirement planning, don't overlook these crucial factors that can greatly increase the amount of money you will need over more years than you expect.

§ 11.6.1.
Many People Are Living Longer

Many people underestimate life expectancy. According to the Social Security Administration, men age 65 today can expect to live until age 83 on average. For women age 65, average life expectancy today is age 85. Since those are averages, half of the people will live past those ages. The Social Security Administration says that about one out of every four 65-year-olds will live past age 90, and one out of 10 will live past age 95[36].

I've met folks who actually spent more years retired than working! If you spend your savings based on planning for a 20-year retirement and then live longer, you'll run out of money and wish you'd erred on the side of caution.

§ 11.6.2.
Inflation and Taxes Can Squeeze Your Income

If you don't factor inflation into your retirement planning, your income will remain level while prices rise. Eventually you'll have to find ways to spend less (lower your standard of living) or you'll deplete your assets faster.

Of course, you can't know what inflation will be during your retirement. Obviously prices tend to go up but by how much? Over the past 100 years, inflation has averaged about 4 percent per year. Even with relatively mild inflation over the past 25 years, the cost of living has more than doubled. And you may recall double-digit inflation from 1977 to 1981, when inflation averaged a staggering 10 percent per year.

Typically, you should plan for 3 to 4 percent inflation. Assuming 3 percent inflation during your retirement, you would need to increase your income and withdrawals each year by 3 percent to maintain your standard of living. So if you need $60,000 in the first year of retirement, you would need $61,800 the second year, $63,654 the third year, and so on. At that rate, after 20 years of retirement, you would need $105,000. After 30 years, it would be $141,393!

Your assumptions for inflation will drive your investment mix. You will need to invest to provide an increasing level of available cash from your investments during retirement. While Social Security includes a cost of living increase, pensions or other income may not, and your annual increases will need to come from good investment decisions.

Keep in mind that your expected rate of return on investments often goes *down* in retirement, as you reposition assets to reduce risk. Since 1926, stocks have averaged about 9 percent rate of return; bonds about 5 percent; and Treasury bills (cash equivalents) about 3.5 percent.[1] With the current interest returns near record lows for recent history, a portfolio built around cash investments (CDs, Treasury bills, and the like) can lose ground to even today's modest inflation. That is why other investments (stocks and bonds) need to be included in the investment mix with caution.

Inflation is why not taking any risk in your investments is risky. The goal is to balance the return you require against the risk resulting from higher-return investments.

§ 11.6.3.
Paying for Your Lifestyle

Don't presume that your cost of living will go down dramatically in retirement. Yes, studies indicate that after retiring, most people can expect to need between 65 percent and 80 percent of their preretirement income to live on each year. However, folks at the lower end of that range are those who were already saving a large portion of their earnings, and who don't have a mortgage, rent, or other debt, or who had very high incomes that supported an expensive lifestyle they don't plan to continue in retirement. But if you've been spending most of what you earn on your current already frugal lifestyle, or you have a mortgage or pay rent, then you should presume your income needs in retirement will be close to what you're already spending (probably closer to 80 percent or more). That means you need to look closely to identify specific expenses that you can (and will) reduce. And be sure to increase your projected cash needs for travel or expensive hobbies that you're planning to do more of in retirement.

§ 11.6.4.
Expect Future Health-Care Needs

Don't overlook how quickly your retirement savings could be drained if you or your spouse has major health-care costs. Even with Medicare, there will be ongoing costs for copays and deductibles for prescription drugs and doctor visits.

If you or your spouse needs long-term care, the costs may shock you. Recent national studies indicate that the national average cost for a semiprivate room in a nursing home is over $80,000 per year and increasing rapidly. The average cost of assisted living is over

$42,000 per year. And the average rate for home health aides is $21/ hour. Someone needing around-the-clock care at home could easily expect to spend $10,000 to $15,000 per month or more depending on the arrangements. Failing to plan ahead for these types of costs means you or your spouse may run out of money—and could leave the surviving spouse nearly penniless for many years.

§ 11.6.5.
Think Twice about Aging in Place

Like most people, you probably want to live out your retirement in your own home. Wanting to age in place is understandable. To make it more likely to happen, you need to plan ahead and understand the costs involved.

For example, carefully consider your current home. Will you be able to maintain it yourself, both the yard and the building? If your home is larger than you need, perhaps downsizing sooner than later makes sense to avoid rising property taxes. Is your home senior friendly? Mobility and joint problems and dangers of falling only get worse over time. Assuming that your home is arranged so you can live on one floor if needed, you may be able to refit your home for senior living. Be sure to factor those costs into your retirement plan. You should find a good contractor and get started. That way you'll have the work completed in advance, before health conditions require quick changes to be made at the last minute.

Some people decide to move from their home, either to be closer to family or to go into a retirement community. In that case, you will incur expenses to get your home ready to sell. That frees your home's equity for retirement. But that is offset by the money you put into a new home or to buy in to the retirement community.

§ 11.6.6.
Helping Out Your Children…and Parents

One of the difficulties of saving for retirement is that many people help out their adult children financially over time, in amounts large and small. If that's you, you'll have to decide whether to stop helping out as much after you retire. Even then, you're likely to dip into your own savings when your children have a financial crisis, such as losing a job or major health issues.

You may also be supporting aging parents. Some retirees I meet with are in their 70s and still caring for aging parents in their 90s. They may even be paying for their parents' cost of care at home or paying for extras in the nursing home that Medicaid doesn't cover. If you're in that situation, you may face difficult decisions especially if your own health declines and your parents appear to be on the road to living to age 100 or more.

§ 11.7.
MISTAKE #5:
IGNORING NONFINANCIAL PLANNING

While this chapter has focused on your retirement finances, other factors are important, too. These nonfinancial considerations can greatly influence your happiness in retirement—and maybe even influence how long you live! Here are some nonfinancial keys to a successful retirement that I've noticed with my clients.

§ 11.7.1.
Stay Connected with Others

People who maintain relationships with others tend to be happier and live longer. For many people, they need to plan to stay involved with family (who may live nearby or at a distance), friends (both old and new), and those they meet through clubs, volunteering, church, or other social activities.

§ 11.7.2.
Do Things You Enjoy

Maybe your vision of retirement has always been to relax and do very little. But do you really want to do nothing for 20 or 30 years? You'll likely become bored, feel out of touch, and neglect your health unless you stay active and involved. Plan to keep a sense of purpose. That may be volunteering for a worthwhile cause or finding work you enjoy even if you don't need the income. You can also dedicate yourself to staying in shape. Being physically fit can directly affect not only how long you live but also how you feel and whether your mind stays sharp. Many studies are finding links between physical inactivity and different types of dementia. As some of my happiest clients tell me, they would rather "wear out than rust out."

Your financial independence in retirement should allow you to spend time doing what you want. After you've got your financial bases covered, don't just stop there. Be sure to include planning for how you really want to spend your time in retirement that is likely to last 20 years or longer.

§ 11.8.
MY WISH FOR YOUR RETIREMENT

In your retirement, here's my wish for you from an old Irish saying.

I wish you health, I wish you wealth, and happiness galore.

I wish you heaven when you die; what could I wish you more?

May your joys be as deep as the oceans, your troubles as light as its foam.

And may you find sweet peace of mind, wherever you may roam.

For more information, visit the website of

The Elderlaw Firm

at **www.elderlawfirm.com**

[33] US Social Security Administration, *When To Start Receiving Retirement Benefits*, SSA Publication No. 05-10147, ICN 480136 (August 2012), http://www.socialsecurity.gov/pubs/10147.pdf

[34] Ruth Helman, Nevin Adams, Craig Copeland, and Jack VanDerhei, "2013 Retirement Confidence Survey: Perceived Savings Needs Outpace Reality for Many," EBRI Issue Brief, no. 384, March 2013, http://www.ebri.org

[35] The following descriptions of the four categories of financial advisors can be found at Financial Industry Regulatory Authority, Inc., *Selecting Investment Professionals*, http://www.finra.org/Investors/SmartInvesting/GettingStarted/SelectingInvestmentProfessional/P117278

[36] US Social Security Administration, *Calculators: Life Expectancy*, http://www.ssa.gov/planners/lifeexpectancy.htm

I SAID MEDIATE NOT MEDITATE!

CHAPTER 12

THE BENEFITS OF ELDER MEDIATION— TO THE FAMILY AND TO THE SENIOR

Terri E. Hilliard Olson, Esquire

Terri E. Hilliard Olson, J.D., spent many years as a civil litigator before founding her estate law and mediation and dispute resolution practice, Hilliard Hopkins, LLP, in Westlake Village, California.

§ 12.1.
INTRODUCTION

This is a story about a family with a "white elephant" in the room.

The parents are seniors. The dad has memory issues, so the couple recently moved to an assisted living facility. Their children are grown. One child experiences Asperger's syndrome, and she's having a tough time making it in the real world. So she now lives in her parents' home...and asks her parents for financial help every month.

The other children aren't in touch with each other very much...or with their parents. However, one of the daughters apparently found out about the parents helping the child who has Asperger's. She's been asking everyone else in the family why the parents are helping that child but not the others. In addition, she's also been asking everyone else why that daughter's been living in the parents' home rent-free in addition to receiving a monthly stipend. Like many adult children, they're concerned with their future roles if their parents eventually need nursing home care and their own roles in paying for that nursing home care.

Now can you see the white elephant in the room? With all this going on, and the dad beginning to lose his memory, there's potential for a genuine "family feud."

The parents came to me for help. They wanted to have a family meeting. The very first thing they told me was that their children wouldn't come. However, when I set up a meeting among all the family members...they all *did* come. As often happens, each child took me aside and apologized in advance for wasting my time, as there was no hope of a resolution. I always smile and say, "No problem. Let's just see what we can do. I am here to help."

Once they actually sat down in the room with their parents and their siblings, these noncommunicative, somewhat resentful family members were all willing to let each other speak, and to listen, for the first time in a long while.

Together, they created a plan to preserve and protect their parents' assets, to control the process, and to assist the daughter with Asperger's to become more independent. With an assist in learning to listen to—and to *hear*—each other, the family was able to understand, to forgive, and to reconcile.

Their plan is now working beautifully. And everyone's happy because everyone's concerns were heard and because they had a structure to manage communication and choice, both now and in the future.

This story has a happy ending. Unfortunately, I hear a lot of stories that don't. So many families are overwhelmed by resentment, long-stifled anger, and perceived slights. So many families end up airing their bitterness out in court, on the public record, on the court's timetable, at costs that are ten or twenty times more than it would cost for a mediator...and none of the parties emerge satisfied. As a result, I see many families that are fractured forever. The seniors go to their graves with the knowledge that the families they loved and raised are no longer intact and are in pain. It is not the legacy they meant to leave their family.

I see them fighting when the parents are alive and when they're dead. I see them fighting over questions ranging from who runs the business, to who gets the money, to who takes the car keys away from Mom. I see them fighting over the mundane and the important.

And, far too often, I see them still fighting the fights that were never resolved years ago.

I believe one of the reasons families fight is because different generations speak different "languages." Think about it for a moment. Don't elders often interpret the same words differently from their boomer children? And don't adult grandchildren often interpret words and meanings differently from their boomer parents, let alone their grandparents?

Sometimes it's not even *words* that are important but the *expectation* that seniors will see things differently and will express these perceptions differently. A good mediator will be aware of these differences as well as any cultural or generational biases among family members and will do his/her best to mediate around them.

Perception, too, is important. For example, some seniors may not speak out about their needs, because (a) they don't want to feel like a burden to their families or (b) they may feel that anything they say will be misunderstood, anyway. But that only adds to the bleeding. After all, we all want choice and control but rarely feel that we can ask for what we need. How can decisions be made for our loved ones if we don't know what *they* have to say, too?

The path can be even trickier if loved ones are a thousand miles away. People are living longer these days, making it more important than ever that family be available to help them. These days, though, it is rare and impractical for generations of the same family to live under the same roof. Or the same town. Or, often, even in the same state.

Interestingly, it's baby boomers who are driving the growth of elder mediation. Why? It's simple. The ways in which they communicate have always been more important to the boomers than to previous generations. They reach out for resources and information. And elder mediation is all about more effective methods of communicating.

As the boomers themselves age and government resources dwindle, many will face difficult choices themselves, in addition to helping their parents make choices. The recent recession drove home a sobering reality to a generation that was brought up to believe they'd have it better than their parents. At an age when their parents were starting to retire, many boomers are working harder (and longer) than ever before. At an age when their parents were finally starting to feel secure, many boomers are more economically insecure than ever. Family strategies will have to be flexible to address changes in family resources. And planning these strategies must take place in advance—not on the fly.

Among the 80,000,000 boomers, elder mediation is becoming the new model for addressing family concerns about their loved ones—and about themselves. Mediation meets the needs of the boomer generation. It's faster, less expensive, less public, less confrontational, and much more likely to bring the family together, rather than split it apart, than any other method of resolving elder care questions.

In plain English, it's quicker, simpler, and easier.

And most boomers—as well as seniors—really could use a little "quicker, simpler, and easier" in their lives!

§ 12.2.
What Is an Elder Mediator?

Elder mediation is the mediation of any conflict involving elders, family members, or other people/institutions in their lives, such as assisted living facilities, health-care providers, caregivers, care managers, financial advisors, and attorneys.

An impartial mediator gathers facts and breaks down barriers to communication. She provides a way out of family stalemates by facilitating discussion among the different parties, by promoting understanding of each other's interests and positions among all parties, by helping the parties focus on the real issues, and by seeking creative solutions that enable the parties to reach agreement.

The mediator doesn't offer opinions and doesn't render decisions. Rather, he/she organizes the discussion and encourages the free exchange of opinions on the key subjects (as opposed to old, irrelevant resentments or issues). This generally enables the parties to arrive at a mutually satisfactory agreement among themselves.

Each person has the chance to address his/her own concerns and needs, so no one feels left out. Most often, the result is that families can talk amongst themselves—productively—in a spirit of openness and cooperation that may not have existed before. Family members can discuss these important issues with a goal of solving them—not rehashing old grudges. For many families, it's the first time they've ever broached the subject. And, for others, it's the first time in years, because they were unable to speak (or listen) cooperatively before, whether out of rancor or simply because the aging of our parents is, by nature, an uncomfortable subject that many of us go to great lengths to avoid.

The goals of mediation?

- A mutually acceptable solution
- Generally, a written agreement (sort of a to-do list)
- If it's a written agreement, one that's binding and enforceable
- To enable the family to avoid litigation and to help them remain a family

For many families, the entire mediation process is a revelation because they never thought they could sit down and discuss these issues in a spirit of give-and-take.

An elder mediator encourages voluntary agreement on the part of the different parties, and in the process, helps keep families together.

However, a mediator's role doesn't have to be restricted only to a reactive mode—after problems pop up! Often, mediation can be most effective *before* something becomes a problem. With advance planning, you're prepared for any eventuality. There are no surprises—everyone knows the scenario in advance. No one can say they weren't told or were kept in the dark. When you plan in advance, there's no such thing as a last-minute crisis. Because, when you're proactive, any problems that crop up can be resolved in a calm and cooperative manner—and they don't become crises.

It's obviously easier to work through elder issues—for example, to discuss care for your parents if they become ill or incapacitated—when people are calm and relaxed.

The mediation approach is confidential, voluntary participation by anyone with a stake in the issue, impartiality, a what-can-be approach (realism!) instead of each person's own interests and what-should-be's, shared and open communication, and problem-solving. This approach dramatically lessens the chances of a back-and-forth blame game or unfortunate words that can never be taken back.

There are two main areas in which elder mediation can help, and most potentially contentious issues fall into these areas. The first area is in planning for your—or your loved one's—inevitable journey down the elder path and for the inevitable physical and emotional changes that will occur on that journey. Basically, we're talking about the eventual possibility of your loved one being unable to live alone – again, choice and control.

Accordingly, children may wish to discuss with their parents issues such as conservatorship of "them," which is the legal authority to make health and welfare decisions; or conservatorship over their assets, in which someone is appointed to make financial decisions. And the family may also wish to discuss a less costly and more private method called powers of attorney. Often, with issues like these, there are ten opinions for every nine people. So it's much better to discuss them *before* they happen than after, when there's a much greater chance that emotion will rule, rather than logic.

The second major area in which mediation can help is the financial/estate planning aspect. The advantage here is that the elder will be able to communicate his plans to his children before they're sitting at a reading of his will. This cuts down on "surprises." And it gives the elder a chance to make adjustments, if he/she is so inclined, before it's too late.

When you really look at it, elder mediation isn't really much different from other types of mediation, except for one thing. In elder mediation, the different "sides" are generally from several generations of the same family.

§ 13.3.
The Benefits of Elder Mediation

One of the reasons I became an elder mediator is that, as an elder law attorney, I saw first-hand many potential problem areas that weren't being addressed or that were being addressed in counterproductive ways, causing untold anguish to both seniors and their families.

I felt there had to be other alternatives to going to court, or to having personal, family issues decided by an arbitrator. And, as you can see, there *is* an alternative. And it works much better for most families.

- Mediation is less expensive than other conflict-resolution methods—especially going to court!
- Mediation is less time consuming. A mediation process can take only weeks…and, sometimes, just days. Arbitration—in which an appointed arbitrator renders a nondisputable decision—takes longer. And a court case can take forever.
- In mediation, the family controls the process, the decision making, and the timing. In litigation, the court will control all of those factors.
- Mediation has the potential to save family relationships and to keep a family together. A court case has the potential to destroy the family.
- Privacy! A mediation process doesn't become public record. A court case does.
- Mediation doesn't present the logistical problems that arbitration or a court case does.

- A mediation agreement—which is agreed upon by all parties—is easy to understand. A court decision? Well, how good's your "legalese?"
- In mediation, the decisions are voluntary. In arbitration, that's not the case. And it's certainly not the case in a court of law, either.
- Nationwide, participants in the mediation process report high degrees of satisfaction with both the process and the results. Again, compare that with arbitration or litigation.
- The first item on this list is worth repeating: Mediation is a fraction of the cost of litigation and significantly less than arbitration.

One of the main bumps in the road is possible age bias, often steeped in different generations of a family. That can be a problem in itself. But combined with other factors such as a family business, the potential for misunderstandings increases measurably. In a family business, some family members may work there or may own shares while, of course, others may not. Also, those family members working in the business probably work harder and put in more hours than the regular workers. As a result, there may be certain expectations on their part—which may not necessarily be shared by the family members running the business.

In addition, if there are several family members in senior positions, they may each have their own visions of how the company should be run after the senior is no longer involved…or no longer around. A good mediator can help bridge the divide between expectations of different family members—and between expectations and reality.

Business is hardly the only area where there can be a big divergence of perceptions and viewpoints. Often, it's simply about the needs of the senior. For example, the mother might be widowed, but she's been in control of her own finances. In many families, there would not have even been a discussion about what happens if Mom gets ill. But there should be; the children could be scattered all over the country, and they also could have their own special situations, such as children who have disabilities.

In cases like these, it's quite common for the expectations on one side of the generational divide to be different from those of the other. Again, mediation is a good way to bridge the differences between expectations.

Many people, unfortunately, call a mediator only after a problem has erupted. However, John A. Gromala, an attorney who helped pioneer the elder mediation movement in America, says its biggest benefit is just the opposite—it can help families avoid ugly disputes in the first place!

"Use of an independent mediator during the planning process," Gromala has written, "can help estate planners improve client satisfaction, reduce the probability of family litigation and avoid malpractice claims. The goal of retaining a mediator in estate planning is to prevent a future problem rather than to solve an existing dispute. If there is current conflict among family members, only mediation offers the probability of a solution that includes reconciliation."[37]

§ 12.4.
THE PROCESS

One of the best things about the mediation process is its simplicity.

First, each person is given a chance to air their views. During this time, no one can interrupt. After each person speaks, the mediator repeats the general tone of what he/she said back to that person and then back to the group.

The facts are gathered, and the issues are identified. Then comes some brainstorming, where common solutions are sought. All options are reviewed. Then it's time for some good old-fashioned horse trading. More often than not, the parties eventually arrive at a mutually agreeable settlement.

Some people feel more comfortable with a written agreement, which each party can then take to his/her own attorney for approval. Others, however, feel it's not necessary to draft a formal agreement. Often it depends on the family dynamics. There's no right or wrong here. "Right" is whatever works.

Often, an attorney drawing up an estate plan will send the parties to a mediator, so all members can potentially "buy in" to the plan. From that point on, mediators and attorneys will work hand in hand to help these clients. This reduces potential conflicts of interest for the attorney. "A mediator recognizes the attorney's lead role and will not question the advice given by an attorney," John Gromala writes. "The mediator's role is to assist attorneys in fulfilling their responsibility to craft a plan that will accomplish the testamentary desires of the attorneys' clients. The mediator confers, on a confidential basis, with each person separately and with the parties jointly. Only information that is authorized to be disclosed by each person will be shared with others. The mediation process can provide attorneys, accountants and financial advisors with valuable information about the clients' subjective interests and needs that should be addressed in the estate plan."[38]

Through it all, the mediator is in control of the process, and the parties are in control of the content and the resolution.

It's all pretty simple.

Here's what one of my clients said about the process:

"My dad was ill with onset of dementia. And my siblings and I hadn't spoken since my mother's funeral four years earlier, when we had bitter disagreements about Dad's care. Through mediation, we were able to reconcile as a family, understand the past decisions, and create a good solution for Dad's care now. It felt like a miracle."
—Jon. H.

§ 12.5.
WHO CAN BENEFIT FROM MEDIATION?

"Concerns about car keys and related issues of driving and transportation, contested guardianships and disagreements about how to care for parents are the most common conflict points in my experience," says Janet E. Mitchell, cofounder of the National Eldercare Mediator Network[39].

But if you think those are the only issues, think again. You can benefit from mediation if

- You have a child who is mentally or physically challenged.[40]
- There's a marked economic disparity among your heirs.[41]
- You are divorced from your children's parent and remarried, and you want to avoid any issues between your second spouse and your children after you're gone.[42]
- You've inherited property or are leaving property.[43]

- One of your children is acting as caregiver to you or your spouse. Does that child deserve more than the others? And how is that going to go over with the others?[44]
- Your testator is very indecisive or too dogmatic.[45]
- You have a family business. Having a family business is like having a bull's-eye on your family's back. That's the kind of thing that can tear a family apart, especially if one or more children are working in the business, and especially if you'd like a certain child to take over the business after you're gone.[46]
- You are probating an estate or administering a trust.
- You are on your second marriage, and you are in a "mixed" or blended family, with children from each spouse, or children brought into the marriage either by you or your second spouse.
- You are *about* to get remarried or involved in a "significant other" relationship.
- You are part of a nontraditional marriage—gay or lesbian, transgender, etc.
- There are questions or issues you've ignored or put off "for later," in the interest of family harmony.
- You—or your family—have questions about housing/living arrangements, health-care planning, financial management, estate planning, medical treatment, guardianship, or conservatorship.
- You are making end-of-life, burial, and funeral decisions.
- There are disputes—or potential disputes—among adult children involving finances or care choices, selling assets, inheritance, your estate, etc.

§ 12.6.
THE RESULT

These are the words of another one of my clients—told to me long before I had ever heard anything about this book, or participating in the writing of it:

"We had a family meeting called by my mother, who wanted to remarry at 85. The mediator was able to help us, as her family, understand her feelings and decision, and for her to understand our concerns. We are all happier because of it, and we are certain it would have not gone well if we hadn't... We have peace of mind." —Sara M.

Every elder law attorney can tell you sad stories about families who kept putting "it" off. We run into people, all the time, who'd like to put it off, to deny, to delay, to wait until "it's time," to wait until "things are better," etc. Inevitably, these people eventually come to the realization that they (or their parents) aren't getting any younger—that family problems generally don't disappear with time; they generally disappear only through action. And that waiting, denying, and delaying only make problems worse.

And that's when they finally decide to be proactive and take the steps now that can prevent a touchy situation from escalating into a bad one and a bad situation from escalating into a horrible one.

As an elder law attorney as well as an elder mediator, I'd like to think that gives me a special insight into the benefits of mediation and effective elder and special needs planning for my clients.

You still need an attorney to effectively plan your (or your parents') estate and to effectively address any changes that may need to be made in the planning. But if you're at all uncertain about what you want, or about the roles of other family members, mediation can be invaluable.

It saves you time, saves you money, saves you aggravation, saves you unwanted publicity from proceedings that become part of the public record, saves you from being at the mercy of the court's schedule rather than your own, saves you from a solution dictated by a third party, and often, can save you a lot of heartache. It will give you peace of mind.

Particularly if you're a boomer, and there are unaddressed aging issues for either your parents or yourself, elder mediation is an idea whose time has come!

For more information, visit the website of

Hilliard Hopkins, LLP,

Estate, Business and Special Needs Planning

at **www.hilliardhopkins.com**

[37] John A. Gromala, J.D., *The Use of Mediation in Estate Planning: A Preemptive Strike Against Potential Litigation*, Academy of Professional Family Mediators (May 1999), http://www.mediate.com/articles/estate.cfm

[38] *Id.*

[39] Parentgiving, Inc., *Elder Mediation: The New Crisis Counseling*, http://www.parentgiving.com/elder-care/elder-mediation-the-new-crisis-counseling-part1/

[40] John A. Gromala, J.D., *The Use of Mediation in Estate Planning: A Preemptive Strike Against Potential Litigation*, Academy of Professional Family Mediators (May 1999), http://www.mediate.com/articles/estate.cfm

[41] *Id.*

[42] *Id.*

[43] *Id.*

[44] *Id.*

[45] *Id.*

[46] *Id.*

IT TAKES A VILLAGE TO CARE FOR A SENIOR

CHAPTER 13

WHY IT TAKES A VILLAGE
TO CARE FOR A SENIOR

Richard R. Vouga, Esquire
& Dana L. Vouga, Certified Senior Advisor

§ 13.1.
INTRODUCTION

The call came at about eight o'clock on a Tuesday night. Our 91-year-old neighbor, Edna, was in the hospital. Walking in the door as she returned home from her weekly bridge game, her brand-new, bells-and-whistles door, with the spring that closes hands-free, slammed her in the backside, knocking her into her kitchen. Thankfully, her friend saw the incident as she was putting her car into reverse and ran to her aid. By the time it all was sorted out and we heard the story, Edna was scheduled for surgery the next morning for replacement of her sheared off hip socket. Her sons sorted out their concerns and fairly negative predictions, and everyone met at the hospital totally unprepared for what they found. Expecting to find their fiercely independent mother bruised, medicated, and out of sorts, they instead found a positive, proactive, motivated woman who was already establishing herself as the decision maker. She was going to start walking in the morning, would have rehab, her insurance would pay for it, and she already had contacted friends and had them bringing her some stuff from home that she wanted. Three weeks of rehab, and then she would be going home...

As we kept tabs on her progress, the family prepared for the conversation that they would surely have to have. How could a woman of her advanced age pull out of this and return to her formerly independent life at her home? Knowing that Edna had singlehandedly cared for her husband for a decade as he declined, finally dying in his bed at home, made the situation even more challenging. Her three sons lived out of town and their wives worked. They were not in a position to provide the level of physical care she might need. Not that she would have wanted to leave her own home, even if they had invited her to stay with them.

Two and a half weeks and several visits later, we continued to be impressed, and at times amused, by Edna's progress. The windowsill of her rehab room was full of baskets of get-well cards from people in her small town. The rehab bedding had been replaced by a powder blue comforter, the hospital gown by much more attractive lounge-wear, courtesy of two friends who were at her beck and call and, in fact, arguing over who could be the most helpful. The kitchen staff had adjusted to her very long list of foods she refused to eat and consented to not deliver a tray of anything to her that she did not like! She was thriving on bananas just the right shade of yellow, and turkey sandwiches on plain white bread. And, even though it was a lot of work, she was the star in rehab. Always one to follow the recipe, she was taking instruction, doing her exercises, using the sock gadget, and asking for help if she needed it. The day had come. The doctor pronounced that Edna could be discharged home. From her rehab room, she had already lined up help. A neighbor girl (she was actually 65, but to Edna, she was a girl) had been asked to come in and help with getting in and out of bed, meals, and driving. Edna would pay her of course but not too much. Another neighbor would help her with chores such as the garden and house cleaning. And so our first experience of Edna needing help played out. There were moments that seemed a little goofy, like when her helper confided that she suspected Edna had driven the car to town and what should be done about it; the time she also was worried that Edna was responding to what appeared to be a scam letter. And the time we visited and found her financials were proudly laid out for the entire world to see. Her friends confirmed that yes, she did show people her investment details and very proudly; and the copy of the hip X-ray she intended to pull from her purse that turned out to be a list of her grandchildren's names, birthdays, and Social Security numbers.

Putting aside their concerns, Edna's family had much to be grateful for in her story. Although she did not end up needing nursing home care, and in fact, could pay reasonable costs for some private help, she had done her estate and long-term health-care planning when she was 84. Her sons were her agents under her durable powers of attorney. Her house and some investments were in an asset protection trust. She was well past the five-year look-back so these assets were fully protected from Medicaid spend down and estate recovery. She had taken advantage of social opportunities in her later years, becoming part of a bevy of card-playing women, most younger than she, who had become friends. They watched out for her too. And she did have investments. Working as a teacher when teachers did not make much money, and married to a farmer who put food on the table and was willing to make do, she had developed a frugal lifestyle and was skilled at improvising. And when she was ready to retire, she sought the help of a financial planner who understood the unique challenges faced by seniors. Her modest estate had grown, and she had saved a real bit of money.

We look at the process of getting older and the many directions life can go. When I think about Edna's experience, it is clear that some proactive choices and key individuals can help make advanced years or a health emergency much more agreeable. The influence of credible people is important in our lives, all of our lives. In the senior years, there is wisdom in appointing a neutral but informed resource toward a solution, and encouraging a relationship with a handful of trusted professionals who may help when a course of action needs to be taken.

So who and what are the human resources that might strengthen the planning, influence the quality of life for seniors, and thereby improve the quality of their relationships with those who care for them? A look at the resources available to help seniors as they age will highlight the village it takes to care for a senior.

§ 13.2.
WHY IT TAKES AN ELDER LAW OR SENIOR ESTATE PLANNING ATTORNEY

Many people believe that the same attorney who helped in a past real estate transaction, or who settled their divorce or neighbor dispute, is also able to help with their estate and long-term care planning. Not every attorney understands trust law, the rules surrounding Medicaid planning, veterans benefits, tax concerns that apply to retirement planning and estate administration, or the planning for wealth protection that affects those who have considerable assets. Just as teachers choose an area of focus, and physicians may have a specialty, so it is in the legal profession.

What should you expect from an elder law or senior estate planning attorney? Individualized planning that utilizes well-designed legal tools appropriate to the needs and goals of the client can be expected. Estate planning documents such as wills, durable powers of attorney, advance directives, various trusts, care agreements, guardianships, and even planning that applies to a person's business interests must be tailored to fit the individual planning needs of the client. Because each person's circumstances are unique, the planning should not have a cookie cutter feel to it. Beware of documents that may be generalized for the masses; these may not accomplish the important goals that should flavor the language of estate planning documents. Through comprehensive planning, the elder law or senior estate planning attorney is able to help clients plan for eventual long-term health-care needs and the changes in circumstances that might result from life events, such as increased or decreased wealth, death, divorce, remarriage, or a child or grandchild who has special needs.

§ 13.3.
WHY IT TAKES A FINANCIAL PLANNER AND A BANK

Many people find value in the services of a money manager throughout their working and investing career. Their financial advisor is aware of their goals and money-making dreams and is aware of the economic conditions that will affect investing. They expect their planner will chart a course using effective investment strategies able to generate financial progress. Others may wait to engage a financial planner until they are older and want financial advice because they are retiring. They may need someone to tell them how to access and manage their retirement accounts, structure their disbursements, and make investments that will last for their lifetime. For these, experience with a financial planner may be limited to an annual company funded retirement account review. This section will discuss considerations when working with a financial planner and how the planner and the attorney work together to accomplish client goals.

According to the Financial Industry Regulatory Authority (FINRA), "Financial Analyst, Financial Adviser (Advisor), Financial Consultant, Financial Planner, Investment Consultant or Wealth Manager are generic terms or job titles, and may be used by investment professionals who may not hold any specific credential."[47] Anyone who looks in a phone book under the appropriate heading will see letters and registrations too varied to comprehend next to the name of the person promoted as a financial planner. It pays to understand the credentials used by a planner you are considering, and to check the planner's track record. There are also differences in the fee systems used, with many options ranging from fee only to commission based, with choices in between. The FINRA website has helpful tips on choosing a financial planner or a money-managing firm, understanding fee options, and clarifying the various credentials.[48] This website may be worth a look since there are very different requirements for each designation. While many people start with a referral from a trusted source, others may not know where to begin choosing a financial planner. To make this easier, the FINRA website also provides information about brokers, including any negatives that may be attached to their record. By following the menu, an investor can get information about a firm's or a broker's credentials and history; this is a valuable tool in a time when investors want to be sure they are hiring only a trustworthy, talented person to manage their funds.[49]

How do the attorney and the financial planner work together to help meet the planning goals of their mutual client when their objectives may be different? While most money managers' overriding interest is in growing and sustaining wealth, the elder law attorney may have a different objective. The elder law attorney's focus may be on protecting the interests of a person who is going to remain in the community while his or her spouse resides in a nursing home. Or the elder law attorney may be concerned about helping clients reduce their estate taxes and protect their income from long-term health-care costs. Special needs planning is yet another area that requires careful consideration by all parties to ensure that the benefits and programs available to a person who has a disability are not lost or diminished. Because both the financial planner and the attorney want to meet their client's goals, they both need to be involved in the planning. By making sure that everyone at the table understands the goal and the reason for any action, the client's best interest is achieved. In addition, a financial resource that should not be overlooked is the client's community bank. While some banks offer a range of financial planning services, many times the bank is able to assist its client and the attorney with simple needs. Services such as establishing trust accounts, providing medallion signature guarantees, serving as trustee of a trust, and providing verification of account information streamline the process of long-term health-care planning.

§ 13.4.
WHY IT TAKES AN INSURANCE PROFESSIONAL

Without clearly understanding all the product details, most people are aware of insurance in general: auto, life, health, short and long-term disability, and even long-term care insurance. A person's approach to insurance can be minimal or very strategic. While one person may just choose to enroll in an employer sponsored life and accident policy and name a beneficiary of choice, another person may use insurance as part of an investment strategy. The financial planner and the attorney each have an interest in the amount and type of insurance that a client has and want to be sure to include this asset in the planning process. For individuals who have high income, long term care insurance may be a tool purchased to help cover the cost of future long- term nursing home or in-home care. In contrast, life insurance can be an economical way to leave an inheritance. Because Medicaid generally considers insurance that has a cash value to be an available asset, insurance policies can be protected by transferring ownership to a suitable trust. Life insurance is a somewhat passive asset until the point of death, which makes it an excellent choice for trust funding. The beneficiary designations of any life insurance policy are important to long-term care planning and to the planning of the money manager. Annuity products may also be useful in Medicaid planning and in trust funding. A Medicaid qualifying annuity may be used to qualify a client for Medicaid and to help pay for the cost of nursing home care.

§ 13.5.
WHY IT TAKES THE VETERANS ADMINISTRATION

Many wartime veterans and their spouses need to know that there are benefits that offer substantial help paying for unreimbursed medical expenses, including nursing home care, assisted living care, or in-home care for those who qualify. Some may be eligible for a service-connected pension. While the attorney planning for their long-term care needs understands the value of benefits and may be certified to help them access their veterans benefits, many people may rely on their county veterans service officer. This individual should be able to discuss benefits, eligibility criteria, programs, services, and supports provided by the US Department of Veterans Affairs (VA). In addition, the veterans service officer is available at no cost to assist in the claims process.

§ 13.6.
WHY IT TAKES A PHYSICIAN

At the point that the body performs less than adequately, and more help from family is needed, daily interactions and the decisions they revolve around can become a source of frustration for the senior, a caregiver, and family. For example, when should one stop driving? What about end-of-life decisions? Enlisting the physician to deliver that news of limitation or help with sensitive discussions may take the burden off of the caregiver or family. When caring for a person who has dementia or Alzheimer's disease, the physician's opinion and testimony about capacity may be important to determine whether a guardianship should be pursued. A respected but neutral physician can deflect some of the emotion that might be reserved for close family members.

§ 13.7.
WHY IT TAKES THE COUNTY OFFICE OF ASSISTANCE

In a crisis, a person may need to pay for the cost of his or her nursing home care by applying for medical assistance. The crisis may be a new health emergency or a situation where funds have been depleted by the costs of a nursing home stay. The expertise of the county office of assistance to process an application for medical assistance may be the lifeline that prevents a family from depleting assets that may be needed by a community spouse. Many people are unaware of the rules related to Medicaid planning and may liquidate assets needlessly. Consulting an elder law attorney in the event of a health-care emergency will make sure your best interest is protected, and the advocacy of the attorney may result in faster, more positive results with the county assistance office.

§ 13.8.
WHY IT TAKES THE AREA AGENCY ON AGING

At the point that nursing home care is needed, an assessment is required to determine the patient's level of care needs. This service may be performed by the area Agency on Aging. In addition, this agency investigates allegations of abuse and neglect, advocates for the elderly, and administers programs such as Meals on Wheels.

§ 13.9.
WHY IT TAKES COMMUNITY-BASED SERVICES

For the caregiver, finding a temporary respite from the challenge of caregiving can be, in itself, a challenge. This section will talk about resources that may be available in the community to provide temporary care, allowing the caregiver to recharge.

Some states have taken advantage of incentives offered by the federal government to develop community-based, comprehensive care provider facilities under the Program of All Inclusive Care for the Elderly (PACE)[50]. If available where a senior is living, a PACE facility provides participants with comprehensive services, both medical and social. Transportation to and from their community homes, medical management, therapy, personal care, social activities, and meals are all provided in a community group setting. Thus, a caregiver would be able to provide care in the nonprogram hours, while weekdays would be spent at the PACE program. A full listing of available PACE programs is available at:

http://www.payingforseniorcare.com/longtermcare/resources/pace_medicare/provider_list.html.[51]

Because not every state offers PACE programs and not every senior meets the eligibility standards for such programs, caregivers may need to look further. Frequently, assisted living facilities or home health providers offer temporary respite for a fee. While there may be a cost involved, the service is an option if a caregiver needs to go on a trip or find a break from their caregiving responsibilities.

Adult daycare refers to a program that provides temporary daytime care for seniors in an out-of-home setting. Unlike the PACE program, or respite found through an assisted living facility, the focus of adult daycare is custodial and recreational. Those participating in adult daycare may find social opportunities, crafts and recreational activities, snacks, meals, and assistance with their daily needs. According to the Administration on Aging, there may be great differences between daycares, ranging from cost to services provided.[52]

Some home care agencies are able to provide temporary, round-the-clock respite care in the individual's home. Ideally, staff are trained in the unique needs of the individual, and agencies understand the need for reliable staff.

For those who are able to participate at the greater level of social and recreational activity that a senior center provides, participation does offer a caregiver a few hours of free time.

§ 13.10.
WHY IT TAKES SOCIAL INTERACTION

Researchers have long suspected that a socially active lifestyle is beneficial as people age. According to a study by researchers at Brigham Young University and University of North Carolina at Chapel Hill, "individuals with adequate social relationships have a 50 percent greater likelihood of survival compared to those with poor or insufficient social relationships."[53] The study further suggests that social relationships deserve the same weight as other indicators commonly considered when planning for longevity. What does this mean to a caregiver? Arranging opportunities for social connections may be as important to a senior as being proactive with heart health; choosing a healthy medication, diet and exercise routine; or controlling the use of drugs and alcohol.

Because each person's personality influences his or her overall comfort with socializing, a caregiver may need to find, or create, opportunities that are a good fit. While one senior might have all the social involvement they want within their extended family structure, another may be much more isolated. One person might enjoy the activities found at a senior center, while another might prefer to chat with others in a breakfast restaurant, a community veterans club, or a lodge. Still another may find connections by volunteering, attending church, or in a part-time job. As a senior becomes less able to get out, or is medically homebound, the caregiver may need to become more involved in arranging social opportunities. Scheduling regular phone calls and visits by family and friends or neighbors may become necessary. If this is not possible, consider requesting visitation through a church or synagogue, a service organization, or hiring companionship though a home help provider. Many seniors find emotional comfort and companionship in keeping a small pet if they are able to care for, and be safe with a pet.

§ 13.11.
WHY IT TAKES HOUSING

Some people have planned to make sure that their home meets their needs at every stage. Others are determined to live in their house as long as they are able, even if their home is not serving them well. Important needs can be ignored by the emotional inability of the senior to consider other housing choices that could make them very happy. Many seniors have accumulated possessions that make the thought of moving overwhelming. Others fear that selling a family home would disappoint family members. Some are afraid to leave the familiar. How can a caregiver help? A senior may find help with a seniors real estate specialist (SRES'). According to the National Association of Realtors, 20 percent of the adults in the United States are over 50 years of age.[54] The SRES® is trained to understand the various housing options available to seniors and is aware of the concerns facing seniors as they age. They can help seniors make choices or line up services that can make their decision making easier, often pulling in other valued perspectives such as senior estate planning attorneys, financial planners, storage and moving professionals, and home renovation resources.[55]

In addition, subsidized housing for seniors is available through the local housing administration. Some senior care communities offer independent living apartments and may have a continuum of care that allows residents to take advantage of assisted living or skilled nursing care as their need for help increases.

§ 13.12.
CONCLUSION

It does take a village and good collaboration to provide for our many needs as we age. Caregivers who are able to take advantage of community resources and understand the inter-workings of such systems may be rewarded with peace of mind and greater satisfaction for themselves and for those under their care.

We have included only a few types of resources available in "the village."

For more information, visit the website of

Vouga Elder Law, LLC

at **www.vougaelderlaw.com**

or call us at **636-394-0009**

[47] FINRA, *Rules and Resources*, http://www.finra.org/Investors/ToolsCalculators/ProfessionalDesignations/RulesandResources/

[48] FINRA, *Selecting Investment Professionals*, http://www.finra.org/Investors/SmartInvesting/GettingStarted/SelectingInvestmentProfessional/

49 FINRA, *FINRA BrokerCheck – Search*, http://brokercheck.finra.org/Search/Search.aspx

[50] Medicaid.gov, *Program of All-Inclusive Care for the Elderly (PACE)*, http://www.medicaid.gov/Medicaid-CHIP-Program-Information/By-Topics/Long-Term-Services-and-Support/Integrating-Care/Program-of-All-Inclusive-Care-for-the-Elderly-PACE/Program-of-All-Inclusive-Care-for-the-Elderly-PACE.html#

[51] PayingForSeniorCare.com, *List of Medicare PACE Programs*, http://www.payingforseniorcare.com/longtermcare/resources/pace_medicare/provider_list.html

[52] US Department of Health and Human Services, Administration on Aging, *Adult Day Care Facts*, http://www.aoa.gov/aoaroot/Press_Room/Products_Materials/fact/pdf/Adult_Day_Care.pdf

[53] Holt-Lunstad J, Smith TB, Layton JB (2010) *Social Relationships and Mortality Risk: A Meta-analytic Review*. PLoS Med 7(7): e1000316. doi:10.1371/journal.pmed.1000316, p. 14, http://www.plosmedicine.org/article/info%3Adoi%2F10.1371%2Fjournal.pmed.1000316

[54] National Association of Realtors, Realtor.org, *NAR Education Matrix*, http://www.realtor.org/edmatrix.nsf/7d546e6838d031e086256fbd0065092d/1112bccfa33fdf88862572bc0075b895

[55] National Association of Realtors, *Why Use an SRES®*, http://seniorsrealestate.sandstormdesign.com/why-use-sres

IT'S IMPORTANT TO PLAN AHEAD
TO ENSURE YOUR LAST WISHES ARE CARRIED OUT

CHAPTER 14

DYING WITH DIGNITY: RETHINKING HOW WE DIE IN AMERICA

Alice Reiter Feld,
Certified Elder Law Attorney by the
National Elder Law Foundation

§ 14.1.
INTRODUCTION

This is a story about my mother, Rose Meister, who passed away on September 3, 2012.

My mother had been failing for a long time. She wasn't ill, just 91 years old and failing. When she could no longer walk, we put her on hospice. At that point, my brother, who lives in New York, asked, "So what are you going to do, medically, to help her?"

He was taken aback when I answered, "Nothing." And so was the doctor, when I gave him the same answer whenever he suggested some measure that might give a "slim hope" of extending her life—but not her quality of life.

The doctor had told me she would die without ever getting out of bed again. And, a few months later, she did. She took one last breath and just passed away–without being fed by tubes; without being hooked up to breathing matchines; without being sedated because of pain; without being uncomfortable; without even one bedsore; and without every realizing she was dying. She died with dignity. And that's the gift I gave her.

My cousin Trish had a different story.

Trish's mother, too, had started that long, slow slide. She was dying, and Trish knew it. The doctors kept suggesting that additional treatments might offer a "slim chance." And Trish kept going along with them, trying whatever she could to prolong her mother's life without realizing that she was destroying her mother's *quality* of life. So her mother died in a sterile, impersonal hospital with feeding tubes sticking out of her body. To this day, Trish has regrets.

When it's *your* time, which way would you rather die? Like my mother? Or like Trish's mother?

To me, as an elder law attorney, the answer seems very simple. But the answer also leads me to another question: Why don't we ever talk about death or about dying?

We are all going to die. It's not like any of us is going to avoid it. It's not like anyone we love is going to avoid it. Yet, we can sure avoid discussion of it.

Death, it seems to me, is simply the final part of life. So why can't we talk about it?

Is it really necessary for so many of us to die in debt (and to burden our families with this debt) because we've been hooked up to breathing machines that keep us "alive"—but don't really allow us to *live?* Is it necessary for so many of us to do this for "the family's sake," when we may actually be ready to go? And is it necessary for so many of us to die in impersonal hospital settings when there are alternatives that can make the process of dying less traumatic for both patient and family?

I think these are questions worth asking.

§14.2.
THE COST OF DYING IN AMERICA

The costs of keeping people "alive" when there's no hope of meaningful recovery are staggering.

- In 2009, Medicare paid out $55 billion for medical bills in the last two months of life.[56]
- It costs up to $10,000 a day to keep a patient—who may have no chance of meaningful recovery—in intensive care, and up to 20 percent of Americans spend their final days in an ICU.[57]
- A vast majority of Americans say they want to die at home—but 75 percent end up dying in a hospital or nursing home, subjected to uncomfortable machines, surgeries, tubes, sedation, or restraints, in order to prolong "life."[58]
- Eighty-five percent of the health-care bills for terminal patients are paid by the government or private insurers…[59] giving both doctors and hospitals more reason to put patients in hospitals.

However, there's another, more benevolent, reason why doctors are often loathe to give up on a patient. Doctors are trained to save lives, not to give up on them. (Of course, these days, there's another reason, too: fear of lawsuits.)

Because of medical advances, our life expectancy has almost doubled over the past century. Perhaps because of this, do we think about prolonging "life" just because we can?

Dr. Elliott Fisher, of Dartmouth Institute of Health Policy, believes that supply drives its own demand. In other words, hospital administrators, in order to pay their bills, have to keep their facilities filled with paying patients. But it's not really the patients who end up paying. It's you and me.[60]

By law, Medicare cannot reject any treatment based upon cost. It will pay up to $65,000 for patients to receive certain chemotherapy drugs, even though they might only extend "life"—if you can call it that—by a month or two.

And when someone is admitted to the hospital, chances are they'll be seen by a small army of specialists who will conduct tests they probably don't need. We've heard of cases, in fact, where terminal patients were seen by *as many as 25 different specialists*—each billing Medicare separately! And who do you think, really, is paying for those Medicare bills?

It's sad that we don't seem to be consulting the most important person in this whole equation: the patient. If you actually ask most patients, they'd rather be at home, even if it means less aggressive care. And they might want to go on hospice. But not enough people, it seems, are asking them.

§ 14.3.
DOES THE TRADITIONAL WAY OF DYING REALLY HELP THE PATIENT?

We can only guess how many patients would prefer to die naturally, rather than stay "alive" artificially another month or two for the sake of their families.

Much of this unnecessary end-of-life treatment is actually harmful to the patient and can cause pain and infection. Once they're in this self-perpetuating cycle of antibiotics, feeding tubes, ICU, and frequent hospitalizations, it's very hard to get out. Physicians, in effect, are interfering with the normal process of dying.

How do we explain the divergence between our wishes and what actually happens to so many of us? "It's the path of least resistance," according to Dr. Elliott Fisher of Dartmouth Institute of Health

Policy. Dr. Fisher says, "It's simply seen as efficient for doctors to manage seriously ill patients in a hospital setting."[61]

Our current system often results in the cruelest irony of all for both patients and their families—false hope. With each new test or procedure proposed by the doctor, the patient probably gets his/her hopes up. And so does the family. But statistics don't lie. Most of the time, the hope is false. But the additional pain, suffering, poking, prodding, cutting, radiating, chemotherapy, and intravenous lines into the patient are not false!

The only thing that false hope does is make the unbearable even worse, by eventually smashing itself against the sharp rocks of reality and by denying the patient the right to die with dignity.

Each of us is entitled to choose. But, first, we have to learn to talk about death.

Ben Franklin was right about death and taxes. We talk plenty about taxes. But mention the word "death," and we turn mute.

I've made up what I call the "Let's Not Talk about Death Checklist":

- Do you avoid thinking about death?
- Do you believe that thinking about death makes it happen?
- Are you superstitious about death?
- Do you think of death as being something that happens to someone else?
- Do you believe that discussing it is bad luck?

If you answered yes to three or more...congratulations! You're a charter member of the Let's-Not-Talk-About-Death Club!

No one's saying this is an easy thing to discuss. But if you know even one person who's been around longer because he didn't discuss it, I'd like to meet him!

Assuming then, that we, rationally, understand we're going to die, the question becomes "How do we want to die?"

Do we want to spend our last days in hospitals, hooked up to machines that breathe for us and feed us, while being given drugs that can only prolong our suffering, not save our lives?

Some of us will die naturally, in a comfortable environment—perhaps our own home—surrounded by family. Others will die in a cold, sterile hospital surrounded by people in white coats whose job it is to keep us breathing as long as possible.

Despite my rather strong language, either way is okay if it's *your* choice! You—and *only* you—have the right to make *your* final choices about *your* final days. It's a right we've given up for too long!

§ 14.4.
IT'S TIME FOR A NEW WAY OF THINKING!

In my practice, I've found that doctors can actually (and unintentionally) be an impediment in helping families deal with death. Despite the fact that we have a 100 percent mortality rate, many physicians seem unwilling to discuss end-of-life care for their patients. I believe they owe it to their patients, however, to deal with death in a realistic manner.

Consider this: Terminal patients actually live a month longer on hospice—where the emphasis is on comfort rather than cure—than they do in hospitals!

Think about the implications. Despite the billions we're spending on keeping terminal patients alive in hospitals, despite the prolonged agony faced by the family...people actually live longer on hospice! And they're dying "better" there, too, with an attentive staff in a homey, non-sterile room, naturally, with dignity and with time to prepare, emotionally and practically.

These people are taking the power away from the doctors and giving it back to themselves and their families.

Unbelievably, though, a good many of the people making these choices for themselves are—doctors! Yes, you heard me right—doctors!

Most doctors wouldn't be caught dead—pardon the expression—doing to themselves what they sometimes do to others. When faced with a terminal illness, they often decline life-prolonging protocols. Apparently, most prefer to die naturally, not hooked up to machines.

You'd think doctors, with their knowledge, would opt for life-prolonging treatment. But it's just the opposite. They know, more than anyone, how patients suffer needlessly. They know, more than anyone, the limits of medicine, and they don't want to suffer that way.

Most doctors agree they wouldn't want life-prolonging measures. Many wear medallions stamped "NO CODE"—a request that other doctors not perform CPR on them. And many have signed advance directives stipulating that they don't want any life-prolonging measures performed if their illness is terminal.[62]

So how can we change this culture of "prolonging life" that isn't really *life*? And how can we change the hypocrisy of the medical profession so that its practitioners offer patients the same opportunity that most apparently choose for themselves?

First, you can choose an elder care physician who's already disposed to those beliefs (and not only for himself!). You should make that choice, if possible, while your loved one is still healthy. Once he/she is ill, it may be too late.

When you have this discussion, remember there's no "God" after the word "Doctor." You have rights! And if your loved one's doctor is unwilling to accept you, find another doctor.

Maybe we need a new way of thinking about the Hippocratic oath. It might not be that hard a sell to doctors since they generally reject life-prolonging procedures for themselves!

§ 14.5.
STOP THE HORROR STORIES—"WE'RE NOT TALKING ABOUT DEATH PANELS!"

We've all heard a lot of horror stories floating around about the possibility of "death panels." But nothing could be further from the truth.

We're actually talking about just the opposite. We're talking about taking the power away from "panels" of doctors who make decisions about a patient without regard for the patient's wishes.

I'm not advocating terminal patients choosing to die. I'm merely advocating that they be given a choice! This fight is about choice, plain and simple. It's not about what you *should* decide. It's about giving you *the right* to decide.

And that's where an advance directive can be a valuable tool. Less than 25 percent of Americans have one.[63] Also, 90 percent of Americans say they want to die at home but only 20 percent do. And there's a direct connection between these statistics.[64]

An advance directive includes a durable power of attorney for financial issues as well as a power of attorney for health issues. Both are critically important, but we will discuss health-care advance directives.

An advance directive can include items such as a power of attorney for health-care decisions, which allows you to designate someone to make health-care choices for you if you're no longer able to make them yourself. It doesn't take effect until you're incapacitated. (In case of changing family circumstances, however, your document can be revoked and rewritten.) Other parts of the directive can be expressed informally in letters or conversations.

An advance directive affords you the opportunity to state whether you'd like to receive life-prolonging procedures and the person who you'd like to express your wishes to medical staff. And it ensures that your wishes will be followed!

Give copies to your physician(s), family, friends, clergy, and attorney. And when you go to the hospital…"don't leave home without it!"

A "Do Not Resuscitate" order is done for terminally ill patients who do not want to be resuscitated, but it's not done by an attorney. It's a physician's directive, used primarily for terminally ill patients.

Some states have an advanced health directive called POLST—Physician Order for Life Sustaining Treatment. This is superior to a vanilla health-care power of attorney because it includes discussions with the doctor in advance of illness.

You may wish to be kept alive as long as possible or to decline all life support. You may want some types of care—pain management, for instance—but not others, which is why it's important to choose an agent who'll honor your wishes.

Doctors are only human. They may have professional or religious reasons for not wanting to comply with a patient's wish to discontinue life support. And they may also fear liability issues from distraught family members.

Legally, though, doctors are obligated to honor your advance directive. If for any reason they can't, they're required to transfer you to another doctor who will.

So, you see, you have more of a voice than you may have thought. There *are* mechanisms by which you can take control of your own destiny.

All you have to do is use them.

§ 14.6.
TWO STORIES

§ 14.6.1.
A Dignified Lady and a Dignified Death

Through our nation's most difficult time—the Depression and World War II—Eleanor Roosevelt was our first lady. And she remained an iconic figure for the rest of her life.

In the fall of 1962, after being ill for two and a half years and enduring weeks of invasive, spirit-draining testing, the 77-year-old Roosevelt was told by doctors that she probably had tuberculosis. Her response stunned them. She didn't ask for aggressive action. She didn't ask for miracle drugs. She didn't ask for more tests.

"I want to go home," she said simply. She told her children the same thing. So a sympathetic doctor sent her home.

A week later, the tuberculosis was confirmed. Her doctors were overjoyed, because TB was considered treatable. But when they told her the good news, they were—again—stunned by her reply. She told them she wanted to remain at home and that she did not wish to be treated medically any more. She told them she was ready to die.

On November 7, 1962, she went into a coma. Three days later, the "First Lady of the World" passed away. But not before writing in one of her final newspaper columns about "the articles of torture"— the tests she had undergone.

Barron H. Lerner, professor of medicine at New York University School of Medicine, recently wrote about Eleanor Roosevelt's last days. "Just because someone is admitted to the hospital or has a condition that can be temporarily ameliorated does not mean that we must blindly forge ahead," Professor Lerner wrote. "There is something to be said for dying at home like Eleanor Roosevelt did—unattached to any machines."[65]

§ 14.6.2.
Cathie's Mom

Cathie's been one of my dearest friends for 25 years through births, deaths, marriages, divorces, runny noses, and chicken pox.

Her mom was diagnosed with Alzheimer's in 2007.

"We started Mom off on 24/7 in-home care," Cathie says. "But the two in-home workers didn't take insurance, and I was paying out of my pocket. My friend Alice (me!) recommended an assisted living facility. She felt it would be less costly and less worrisome for me if the aides never showed up. But I didn't listen."

Eventually, Cathie began to notice that her mother was sleeping a lot more.

"But I didn't want to put her in an assisted living facility," Cathie says. "I didn't think we could afford it because I was already running out of money. And, to tell you the truth, I felt guilty about sending her there, that I'd be throwing her to the wolves."

Eventually Cathie agreed with me that it was time to move her mom to an assisted living facility (ALF).

"It was ten times better than keeping her at home," says Cathie. "There were only twenty patients, and the care was excellent. And I realize now that I should have put her in there sooner."

Two years later, Cathie's mom fractured her femur without even falling. When they operated, they discovered the reason the bone had cracked. She had bone cancer.

It wasn't easy for me to tell Cathie that her mother should not go back to the ALF. I told her to realize that her 88-year-old mother had advanced Alzheimer's; she didn't even know who Cathie was. I told her there was probably no cure for the bone cancer other than amputation, not a consideration for an 88-year-old woman. And then I told her the hardest thing of all.

"Your Mom's dying," I said.

The doctor backed me up. He told Cathie that her mother would not leave the hospital. But Cathie didn't want to hear it. So she put her mother in a nursing home, even though she was clearly nearing the end.

"The doctors told me a blood transfusion might buy a little time,'" Cathie says. "So I gave them the okay. I just didn't want to let her go."

So Cathie's mom was brought back to the hospital for a transfusion. At this point, even Cathie's 26-year-old daughter, Heather, said to her, "Let her be at peace."

A month later, the doctors said her mother needed another transfusion. This time, finally, Cathie said no.

"Then I went to my mom," she says, "and I told her to do what she needed to do, to be with my father. I don't even know if she heard me. But I had realized that Alice was right. I had been keeping her alive for me, not for her."

Cathie's mother died on November 20, 2012.

"Now I feel that letting her go was good. I feel relieved," Cathie says. "She was finally able to die with dignity. I'm glad I decided not to torture her any longer."

§ 14.7.
WHAT IS HOSPICE? AND WHEN DO WE CALL THEM?

We don't have a choice about dying.

However, we do have a choice about *where* we die. We have a choice about whether we pass away in a hospital, poked and prodded until our last minutes on Earth or if we die on hospice.

Unfortunately, too few of us actually take advantage of hospice because too few of us really understand what it is.

"Hospice" sounds like "hospital." But the resemblance ends there! Hospice serves only terminally ill patients and their families. And it does so with warmth and compassion.

Hospice provides a holistic approach to pain management, through emotional and spiritual care as much as physical. It provides a comforting, warm atmosphere in which the patient can spend his/her final days. And it can even bring that atmosphere to the patient's home or long-term care facility. There's no attempt at cure. Instead, there's a focus on pain relief and affording the patient the chance to die with dignity.

When a physician determines that a patient has six months or less to live, he may call in hospice. At that point, the focus of medical treatment changes from cure to comfort, pain relief, and the dying process for the family as well as the patient. The hospice team (generally a chaplain, certified nursing assistants, a doctor, registered nurse, and social worker) then creates a palliative care plan, in coordination with the personal physician.

Hospice care focuses on "dying well." Team members help patients and families plan the end of life, deal with emotions like fear and grief, and reach closure on issues important to the patient. And they also help ensure compliance with the patient's advance directives.

Hospice is focused on improving remaining life, rather than prolonging it, and on the patient's and family's emotional needs. Hospice even provides grief counseling after the patient passes, helping many people get back to the process of living again.

And there's no cost; hospice care is provided under Medicare.

§ 14.8.
WHAT IS PALLIATIVE CARE?

Palliative care is the prevention and treatment of pain. It doesn't aim to cure. And although anyone can receive it, it is most often associated with hospice.

Palliative care in hospice usually involves a team of specialists to treat pain and clergy to provide emotional support. And it works; studies by Brown University researchers and others have found that families whose relatives died in hospice are more satisfied with care than those whose loved ones passed away in hospitals.[66]

We think of a loved one's death as the worst thing that could happen. But I would suggest that there's one thing even worse—a loved one dying badly. What do we mean by "badly?"

According to Dr. Ira Byock, Director of Palliative Medicine at Dartmouth-Hitchcock Medical Center in New Hampshire, dying badly is "Dying suffering. Dying connected to machines." Dr. Byock believes that if we deny an imminent death, we can become delusional and can start acting in ways that can actually harm our loved one.[67]

When my mom passed away on hospice, I can remember feeling a sense of relief, relief that the long downward slide for her was over, relief that she—who had a deep fear of death—never really understood she was dying, relief that she died peacefully, in no pain, without being force-fed medicine that would only prolong her—and our—pain. We were relieved that she died with dignity, in the comforting setting of hospice.

§ 14.9.
WHAT THE EXPERTS SAY

The following letter to the editor appeared in *The New York Times* in April 2011,[68] in response to a news article:

Re "Hospital Care at Life's End: A Disparity" (news article, April 12):

That more chronic patients die in New York City area hospitals than anyplace else in the country, some 40 percent compared with 28 percent nationally, should be a clarion call for needed change in patient-centered medical practice.

Partly because of the absence of good, comprehensive and timely discussions with patients and their families about palliative and hospice care and referrals to such care, only about 25 percent of those who die in New York are enrolled in hospice compared with the national average, 42 percent.

In New York State, the Palliative Care Information Act, effective in February, is a needed catalyst for change. A model for the nation, the law requires that terminally ill patients be offered information and counseling on appropriate palliative care and end-of-life options, including hospice, and the risks and benefits of those options. The law will result in more and earlier palliative care and hospice referrals.

Evidence shows that when offered, patients choose palliative and hospice care over aggressive hospital interventions, have a better quality of life and may even live longer. And costs at the end of life are significantly reduced.

DAVID C. LEVEN
Executive Director, Compassion and Choices of New York
New York, April 14, 2011

If you'd like your loved one to die with dignity and you want to leave the decision up to him or her instead of doctors, you should consider hospice when the time comes.

We can't choose *when* we are going to die. But we can certainly choose *how*.

It's up to us to make that choice.

For more information, visit the website of the
Law Offices of Alice Reiter Feld & Associates
at **www.florida-elderlaw.com**

[56] CBSNews, *The Cost of Dying: End-of-Life Care* (updated Aug. 6, 2010), www.cbsnews.com/8301-18560_162-6747002.html

[57] *Id.*

[58] *Id.*

[59] *Id.*

[60] Elliott S. Fisher et al., *Slowing the Growth of Health Care Costs—Lessons from Regional Variation*, The New England Journal of Medicine (Feb. 26, 2009), http://www.nejm.org/doi/full/10.1056/NEJMp0809794

[61] Healthy Lifestyle, *End of Life Care: Hopeful Recovery, Or False Hope?* (July 16, 2011), http://www.healthcareplaza.net/end-of-life-care-hopeful-recovery-or-false-hope/

[62] Ken Murray, *The Guardian, How Doctors Choose to Die* (Feb. 8, 2012), available at http://www.guardian.co.uk/society/2012/feb/08/how-doctors-choose-die

[63] Christine Westphal & Teresa Wavra, American Association of Critical-Care Nurses, *Acute and Critical Care Choices Guide to Advance Directives* (Sept. 2005), p. 10, http://www.scribd.com/doc/159374461/Acute-and-Critical-Care-Choices-to-Advance-Directives

[64] Shojania KG, Duncan BW, McDonald KM, et al., eds., *Making Health Care Safer: A Critical Analysis of Patient Safety Practices*, p. 558, Evidence Report/Technology Assessment No. 43 (Prepared by the University of California at San Francisco–Stanford Evidence-based Practice Center under Contract No. 290-97-0013), AHRQ Publication No. 01-E058, Rockville, MD: Agency for Healthcare Research and Quality. July 2001, http://www.ncbi.nlm.nih.gov/pubmed/11510252

[65] Barron H. Lerner, The HuffingtonPost.com, Inc., *What Can We Learn From Eleanor Roosevelt's Death?*, (posted Oct. 23, 2012), http://www.huffingtonpost.com/barron-h-lerner/eleanor-roosevelt-end-of-life-care_b_2006247.html

[66] Peter Waldman, Bloomberg.com, *Preparing Americans for Death Lets Hospices Neglect End of Life* (July 22, 2011), http://www.bloomberg.com/news/2011-07-22/preparing-americans-for-death-lets-for-profit-hospices-neglect-end-of-life.html

[67] CBSNews, *The Cost of Dying: End-of-Life Care* (updated Aug. 6, 2010), www.cbsnews.com/8301-18560_162-6747002.html

[68] David C. Leven, Letter to the Editor, *Hospice vs. Hospital,* The New York Times (Apr. 14, 2011), http://www.nytimes.com/2011/04/19/opinion/l19hospital.html?_r=0